Student Teaching in Your First Inclusive Classroom is an indispensable, practical, and comprehensive resource that addresses critical needs within teacher education programs. Preservice general educators in our program consistently ask for more training in and support for meeting the needs of students with disabilities in their classrooms and creating environments that work for all their students. I can't wait to use this amazing book in my classes!

Susannah Everett, *Associate Professor in Residence, University of Connecticut, USA*

VanLone and Robbie offer an up-to-date much-needed comprehensive guidebook for student teachers and their mentors. How I wish I had had access to such a roadmap—I would have been spared a lot of angst! Clearly and explicitly grounded in research, the guide is rich with examples and specific tips. From the inclusive classroom to the policy world—tomorrow's teachers are well served by this articulate and practical roadmap.

Jane E. West Ph.D., *Education Policy Consultant, Washington, D.C.*

Student Teaching in Your First Inclusive Classroom

As the first inclusive classroom guide for student teachers specifically, this book provides essential support as you navigate your student teaching placement and build the skills you need to support all students. With a focus on how you can effectively apply high-leverage practices in inclusive K-12 classrooms, the book covers a range of relevant topics including: how to understand the needs of students in an inclusive classroom, differentiated lesson planning and delivery, implementing evidence-based instructional and classroom management practices, carrying out individualized education programs, providing appropriate accommodations and modifications, and collaborating with other educators and families. Each chapter features suggestions for online resources, classroom activities to try, and questions for your own self-reflection, making this book a key resource for pre-service teachers working to obtain elementary or secondary teacher certification, as well as their university supervisors and cooperating teachers.

Janet VanLone, Ph.D. is an Associate Professor of Education at Bucknell University in Lewisburg, PA.

Karen Robbie, Ph.D. is a Research Associate at the University of Connecticut in Storrs, CT.

Other Eye on Education Books Available from Routledge
(www.routledge.com/eyeoneducation)

The Co-Teaching Power Zone
A Framework for Effective Relationships and Instruction
Elizabeth Stein

Optimizing Early Auditory Development for Communication and Education
Strategies for Ages 0–8
Kimberly A. Boynton and Darah J. Regal

A New Vision for Early Childhood
Rethinking Our Relationships with Young Children
Noah Hichenberg

Unpacking Privilege in the Elementary Classroom
A Guide to Race and Inequity for White Teachers
Jacquelynne Boivin and Kevin McGowan

Reimagining the Role of Teachers in Nature-based Learning
Helping Children be Curious, Confident, and Caring
Rachel Larimore and Claire Warden

Teaching Higher-Order Thinking to Young Learners, K–3
How to Develop Sharp Minds for the Disinformation Age
Steffen Saifer

Promoting Language and Early Literacy Development
Practical Insights from a Parent Researcher
Pamela Beach

Student Teaching in Your First Inclusive Classroom

A Comprehensive How-to Guide

Janet VanLone and Karen Robbie

Routledge
Taylor & Francis Group

NEW YORK AND LONDON

Designed cover image: Getty Images

First published 2026
by Routledge
605 Third Avenue, New York, NY 10158

and by Routledge
4 Park Square, Milton Park, Abingdon, Oxon, OX14 4RN

Routledge is an imprint of the Taylor & Francis Group, an informa business

© 2026 Taylor & Francis

The right of Janet VanLone and Karen Robbie to be identified as authors of this work has been asserted in accordance with sections 77 and 78 of the Copyright, Designs and Patents Act 1988.

All rights reserved. No part of this book may be reprinted or reproduced or utilised in any form or by any electronic, mechanical, or other means, now known or hereafter invented, including photocopying and recording, or in any information storage or retrieval system, without permission in writing from the publishers.

Trademark notice: Product or corporate names may be trademarks or registered trademarks, and are used only for identification and explanation without intent to infringe.

Library of Congress Cataloging-in-Publication Data
Names: VanLone, Janet author | Robbie, Karen author
Title: Student teaching in your first inclusive classroom :
a comprehensive how-to guide / Janet VanLone and Karen Robbie.
Description: New York, NY : Routledge, 2026. |
Includes bibliographical references.
Identifiers: LCCN 2025016925 | ISBN 9781032731094 hardback |
ISBN 9781032727448 paperback | ISBN 9781003426738 ebook
Subjects: LCSH: Student teaching--United States |
Inclusive education--United States
Classification: LCC LB2157.U5 V28 2026 |
DDC 370.71/173--dc23/eng/20250616
LC record available at https://lccn.loc.gov/2025016925

ISBN: 978-1-032-73109-4 (hbk)
ISBN: 978-1-032-72744-8 (pbk)
ISBN: 978-1-003-42673-8 (ebk)

DOI: 10.4324/9781003426738

Typeset in Palatino
by KnowledgeWorks Global Ltd.

Contents

Meet the Authors xiii
Contributor Bio xiv
Acknowledgments xv

Introduction 1

1 Student Teaching in the Inclusive Classroom 3
   What Is the Inclusive Classroom? 3
   High-Leverage Practices for Inclusive Classrooms 5
   Who's Who in Student Teaching? 5
   Getting the Most Out of Student Teaching 8
      Becoming a Reflective Practitioner 8
      Developing Resilience: Learning from Challenges 9
      Keeping Yourself Afloat 9
      Self-Awareness and Stress Management during Student Teaching 9
   Perspectives in Practice: Raven's First Day 12
   Mentorship Corner: Getting Off to a Good Start 13
      Tips for Cooperating Teachers 13
      Tips for University Supervisors 13
   Practice and Reflect: Application Activities to Support Your Development 14
   Teacher Toolbox: Resources for Further Exploration 15
   References 15
   Appendix A: Introductory Triad Meeting 16

2 The Inclusive Classroom 18
   Looking Back: A Brief History of the Inclusive Classroom 19
   What's Needed for Successful Inclusion? 20
   Getting to Know Special Education Law 23

IEP Basics for Student Teachers 23
    Who's Who on the IEP Team? 23
    The Process: Pre-referral, Referral, and Evaluation 25
    What Happens Next? 25
    What to Expect at an IEP Meeting 26
    Time to Implement! Putting the IEP into Practice 28
Perspectives in Practice: A First-Year Teacher Prepares for a First IEP Meeting 29
Mentorship Corner: Strengthening Understanding of the Special Education Process 30
    Tips for Cooperating Teachers 30
    Tips for University Supervisors 31
Practice and Reflect: Application Activities to Support Your Development 31
Teacher Toolbox: Resources for Further Exploration 32
References 33

3 The Classroom Environment............................35
Why Positive, Predictable, Safe Learning Environments? 36
Background Considerations for SEB Support Practices 37
    MTSS/PBIS Framework 37
    Cultural Responsiveness 37
Establish a Positive, Predictable Learning Environment 38
    Cultivate Positive Relationships 38
    Promote Predictability and Structure 39
Identify, Teach, Prompt, and Reinforce Common Expectations 42
    Identify Common Expectations 42
    Teach Explicitly 43
    Prompt and Reteach Frequently 43
    Reinforce the Use of Expectations 44
Respond Instructionally to Behavior Errors 47
    Considerations for Responding to SEB Errors 49
    Implicit Bias and Disproportionate Discipline 50
    De-escalation Strategies 52
Perspectives in Practice: Stepping into the Role and Promoting a Welcoming Classroom Environment 54

Mentorship Corner: Setting Everyone Up for Success 55
    Tips for Cooperating Teachers 55
    Tips for University Supervisors 56
*Practice and Reflect: Application Activities to Support Your
    Development* 56
Teacher Toolbox: Resources for Further Exploration 57
References 58

4 Positive Student Behavior Support Practices 62
    *Why Do We Need to Know How to Support Students with
        Advanced SEB Support Needs?* 63
    Background Considerations for Advanced SEB Support 63
        Educator Fidelity Matters 63
        Behavior Is Contextual 65
    Basic Behavioral Theory 66
        Three-term Contingency Model 66
        Consequences: Reinforcing or Punishing? 66
        Function of Behavior 67
        Performance or Skill Deficit? 69
    Supporting Students Who Need Advanced Behavior Support 71
        Tier 2 Support 71
        Tier 3 Support 72
    *Perspectives in Practice: Advice on Establishing Yourself in the
        Classroom from a Cooperating Teacher's Perspective* 77
    *Mentorship Corner: Supporting Competency with Positive
        Behavior Support Practices* 78
        Tips for Cooperating Teachers 78
        Tips for University Supervisors 79
    *Practice and Reflect: Application Activities to Support Your
        Development* 79
    Teacher Toolbox: Resources for Further Exploration 79
    References 81

**5 Planning for Effective Instruction in
    the Inclusive Classroom** 83
    Planning for Effective Instruction 84
        Backward Design 85

Explicit Instruction 87
Universal Design for Learning 90
Perspectives in Practice: A Mentor Teacher Guides Inclusive Lesson Planning 93
Mentorship Corner: Supporting Effective Instructional Planning 94
  Tips for Cooperating Teachers 94
  Tips for University Supervisors 95
Practice and Reflect: Application Activities to Support Your Development 95
Teacher Toolbox: Resources for Further Exploration 96
References 97
Appendix A: Lesson Plan Template 98
Appendix B: Lesson Preparation Template (For Scripted Lessons) 99

6 Instructional Delivery and Engagement in the Inclusive Classroom..........................101
Instructional Delivery 102
  Setting the Stage 102
  Active Participation 103
Teaching Practices in the Inclusive Classroom 106
  Giving and Receiving Feedback 106
  Scaffolding 109
  Pacing 110
  Observation and Reflection 111
Perspectives in Practice: Developing Self-Reflection through Journaling 113
Mentorship Corner: Supporting Effective Delivery 115
  Tips for Cooperating Teachers 115
  Tips for University Supervisors 116
Practice and Reflect: Application Activities to Support Your Development 116
Teacher Toolbox: Resources for Further Exploration 117
References 117
Appendix A: GoReact Sample Assignment 119

Appendix B: Classroom Analysis: Lesson Delivery 120
Appendix C: Classroom Practices Video Self-Analysis Guided Reflection Tool 121

7 Collaboration in and Beyond the Classroom 126
Collaboration Is Necessary for Positive Outcomes 126
Collaboration with Colleagues 128
   Teams and Professional Learning Communities 128
   Special Educators 129
   Paraprofessionals 131
   Families 132
Stepping into the Field of Education 134
   Professional Organizations 134
   Policy and Advocacy 134
A Getting Started Checklist for Student Teacher Advocacy 136
Perspectives in Practice: Professionalism Beyond the Classroom 137
   Supporting Your Student Teachers Beyond Your Classroom 137
   Recognizing Problems and Using Your Voice 137
Mentorship Corner: Supporting Effective Collaboration 138
   Tips for Cooperating Teachers 138
   Tips for University Supervisors 139
Practice and Reflect: Application Activities to Support Your Development 139
Teacher Toolbox: Resources for Further Exploration 140
References 141

8 Navigating Challenges and Looking Ahead 144
Common Challenges 145
   Classroom Management 145
   Embracing Feedback and Filtering Criticism 146
   Managing Relationships 147
   Stress and Burnout Management 148
That's a Wrap! 151
   Final Reflection 151
   Building Your Professional Portfolio 151

    Tips for Creating Your Professional Portfolio 152
    Expressing Your Gratitude and Celebrating Success 152
*Finding Your First Teaching Position in the Inclusive
    Classroom 153*
    Obtaining Your Teacher Certification 153
    Job Search Strategies 154
    Job Search Q&A 155
Takeaways for a Successful First Year 159
*Perspectives in Practice: A Novice Teacher on the Importance
    of a Predictable, Welcoming Learning Environment 161*
Mentorship Corner: Supporting a Successful Transition 162
    Tips for Cooperating Teachers 162
    Tips for University Supervisors 163
*Practice and Reflect: Application Activities
    to Support Your Development 163*
Teacher Toolbox: Resources for Further Exploration 164
References 165
*Appendix A: Classroom Practices Implementation Plan:
    Reminders for Starting Your Teaching Career 167*

Meet the Authors

Janet VanLone, Ph.D. is an Associate Professor of Education at Bucknell University in Lewisburg, PA. She holds degrees in Educational Psychology and Special Education (Ph.D. University of Connecticut). Prior to pursuing her doctoral degree, she worked as a special education teacher in inclusive classroom settings and has experience teaching and supervising student teachers at the early childhood, elementary, and secondary school levels. She teaches courses in Educational Psychology, Assessment, Classroom and Behavior Management, and Explicit Instruction and Structured Literacy. In an effort to increase teacher retention and quality, Dr. VanLone studies effective practices in teacher preparation, and how to best support the transition from pre-service to early career. Specifically, she conducts research on the effects of technology-supported interventions, such as video self-analysis, on pre-service teachers' use of evidence-based classroom management practices. She also has expertise in the implementation of positive behavior supports.

Karen Robbie, Ph.D. is a Research Associate at the University of Connecticut focused on supporting Positive Behavior Interventions and Supports (PBIS) at a national, regional, and state level. As a long-time elementary teacher in inclusive classrooms, Karen centers her work on bridging the gap between research and practice. Her research interests include supporting pre-service and early career teachers' implementation of the PBIS framework in classrooms. Additionally, Karen provides professional development and technical assistance to schools and districts throughout the Northeast. Karen serves on several national, state, and local committees focused on promoting positive student outcomes and effective school environments.

Contributor Bio

Marina Ferro is an undergraduate student at Bucknell University majoring in Psychology and East Asian Studies. Marina is a part of Bucknell's Presidential Fellows Program, through which she found the opportunity to work on this textbook. As Presidential Fellow, she is interconnected with a highly intellectual community and works on faculty-led research projects. Marina's previous research and volunteer experiences, including working with children at a daycare and with those with Autism Spectrum Disorder, have made her passionate about inclusivity and equity in classroom environments. Upon graduation, Marina will pursue her Master's in Mental Health Counseling, working toward licensure as a counselor for minorities and marginalized communities.

Acknowledgments

To all teachers—past, present, and future—this book is for you.

To those who taught us, inspiring curiosity and possibility.

To those who teach now, navigating challenges with dedication, creativity, and care.

To those who will teach, stepping forward with hope and commitment to shaping the next generation.

Your work is invaluable. Your impact is immeasurable. Your passion makes a difference every single day.

Thank you.

Introduction

Stepping into the classroom as a student teacher is an exciting and transformative experience. It is a time of immense learning, professional growth, and personal discovery. For those preparing to teach in inclusive classrooms—where students with diverse abilities and needs learn alongside one another—the journey is both rewarding and complex. This book is designed to guide you through that journey.

This book is a resource for three key stakeholders: student teachers, cooperating teachers, and university supervisors. Each plays a crucial role in the student teaching experience, and this book offers practical strategies, mentorship insights, and real-world perspectives to support everyone involved. This book can also be used to mentor new teachers who are completing teacher apprenticeship programs and other alternative pathways to certification.

We begin by setting the stage for student teaching in the inclusive classroom—defining what inclusion means, introducing key players, and offering advice for making the most of this formative experience. From there, we explore the foundations of inclusive education, including special education law, IEPs, and collaboration with colleagues and families. The book also delves into essential teaching practices, such as creating a positive classroom environment, implementing effective behavior support, and designing engaging instruction using frameworks like Universal Design for Learning and Explicit Instruction.

Each chapter includes:

- **Perspectives in Practice**, offering real-world experiences from student teachers, mentor teachers, and first-year educators.
- **Mentorship Corner**, with tailored advice for cooperating teachers and university supervisors to support student teachers effectively.
- **Practice and Reflect**, featuring hands-on application activities to reinforce key concepts.
- **Teacher Toolbox**, providing curated resources for deeper exploration.

The final chapter focuses on wrapping up student teaching, navigating job searches, and preparing for the first year in the classroom. Teaching is a lifelong journey, and we hope this book serves as a foundation for building confidence, competence, and a commitment to inclusive education.

Whether you are about to begin your student teaching experience, mentoring a future educator, or supervising their progress, this book is here to support you every step of the way. Let's get started!

1

Student Teaching in the Inclusive Classroom

It's the start of a new semester at Green State University, and Christian, an undergraduate teacher certification student, is preparing for student teaching at West Lake Middle School. While he feels prepared and has been looking forward to student teaching, Christian is also feeling a little nervous for the first day of school. He wonders if he and his cooperating teacher will have a good rapport. He hopes everything goes well when he is observed by his university supervisor. Will he be able to manage all of the daily tasks, from lesson planning to grading? And, what if the students misbehave when his cooperating teacher leaves the room?

Welcome to student teaching! This is an exciting semester, when all your preparation gets put into practice. It's very common for new student teachers to be feeling a range of emotions, like Christian. Let's face it. While teaching can be a very rewarding career, there are many challenges along the way—especially for novices. The goal of this book is to help you become an effective, confident student teacher who will have a successful early career in education.

What Is the Inclusive Classroom?

In 1975, the United States Congress passed PL 94-142, or the Individuals with Disabilities Education Act (IDEA). Until the early 1970s, there was little legislation requiring US public schools to appropriately include and educate children with disabilities. When passed, IDEA made significant changes to the way we educate students with disabilities, requiring public schools to provide every student identified for special education services with a "free appropriate public education" in the "least restrictive environment." In other words, IDEA ensured that students with disabilities had the right to be educated with non-disabled peers in general education classrooms to the maximum extent possible, as determined by a team of education professionals. Today, approximately 65% of students with disabilities spend over 80% of their school day in general education settings (Rodriguez & Murawski, 2020).

In addition to students with disabilities, general education teachers have students with other diverse learning needs. Linguistic diversity is increasing in the United States, and over five million students in the United States are classified as English Learners (McFarland et al., 2019). According to the National Center for Gifted Children, approximately 6% of students are enrolled in gifted and talented programs. Many K-12 students struggle with mental health issues, have experienced traumatic life events, have been homeless, or are living in poverty. These are complex problems, and improving outcomes for students with diverse needs requires both resources and a research-based, multi-faceted approach. This approach should include improved support for general education teachers' knowledge as well as emphasis on applying effective practices in inclusive classrooms.

Key Takeaways

- *General education classrooms are increasingly diverse and include students with exceptionalities, struggling learners, and students from culturally and linguistically diverse backgrounds.*
- *A well-prepared general education teacher needs to be equipped with the knowledge and skills to teach and adequately support ALL students.*
- *Teacher preparation is vital to both student success and early career teacher success; a high-quality student teaching experience can serve as a buffer against burnout and early career attrition.*

High-Leverage Practices for Inclusive Classrooms

The Council for Exceptional Children (CEC) in partnership with the Collaboration for Effective Educator Development, Accountability and Reform Center (CEEDAR) has identified high-leverage practices (HLPs) for inclusive classrooms (McLeskey et al., 2019). Twenty-two HLPs are organized into four key areas, including collaboration, assessment, social/emotional/behavioral, and instructional practices.

We do not intend to review in detail each specific HLP; rather, we will connect specific topics in the following chapters to HLPs and provide ideas and resources that support student teachers' successful implementation of relevant HLPs. While this book focuses on HLP implementation in inclusive classrooms, we recognize that teacher preparation programs commonly organize student teaching experiences around state teacher preparation standards and competencies. University personnel can complete a crosswalk between HLPs, specific program learning goals, and state teacher preparation competencies to ensure alignment and completeness of the student teaching experience.

Who's Who in Student Teaching?

Many states require pre-service teachers to complete a semester of student teaching, which is commonly a culminating experience for students enrolled in a teacher certification program. Traditionally, there are three key players who are most involved in student teaching. First, of course, is the student teacher. Student teachers can be either undergraduate or graduate students enrolled in a teacher certification program, and programs vary in terms of the length of student teaching; some require a traditional full-time semester, while others offer a year-long teacher residency option. Regardless of the program, a student teacher has a number of fundamental professional responsibilities. Table 1.1 provides an overview of those responsibilities.

Whatever the pathway, student teachers receive guidance, feedback, and mentorship from two additional key players:

TABLE 1.1 Student Teaching Responsibilities

	Student Teacher
Be Informed	• Clearly communicate with cooperating teacher and supervisor • Ask questions to clarify what is expected of you • Understand all requirements outlined by your preparation program
Be Prepared	• Maintain an organizational system for lesson plans • Share lesson plans with cooperating teacher for feedback • Use feedback to inform planning and instructional delivery
Be Professional	• Attend school regularly and be on time • Maintain a professional disposition • Build rapport with staff and students, yet maintain boundaries • Support the overall mission of the school

the cooperating teacher and the university supervisor, who work together to provide the student teacher with experiences, guidance, and feedback that will have them well-prepared for their early career. The cooperating teacher plays a central role in this process, and agreeing to mentor a student teacher is a major professional commitment. While the cooperating teacher's first responsibility is to their school community and their students in the classroom, they must also invest a great deal of experience, patience, thought, and time into developing and mentoring a student teacher.

The university supervisor serves as the bridge between the student teaching experience and the teacher preparation program. This person typically visits the student teacher to observe teaching and provide post-observation performance feedback. The university supervisor should have a broad understanding of all expectations outlined by the teacher preparation program and state department of education. In addition to ongoing observations, the supervisor provides support to the cooperating teacher and addresses any placement-related issues as they arise. Table 1.2 outlines the responsibilities of both the cooperating teacher and the university supervisor when supporting the implementation of HLPs in the inclusive classroom.

TABLE 1.2 Mentor Responsibilities

	Cooperating Teacher	University Supervisor
Primary Responsibilities	• Understand state and university policies and requirements for student teaching and the role of the cooperating teacher • Inform student teacher of school- and classroom-related policies; review teacher-related classroom responsibilities • Provide ongoing guidance and feedback on lesson planning and delivery • Help student teacher become a part of the larger school community	• Understand state and university policies and requirements for student teaching and the role of the supervisor • Serve as liaison between university and placement and work to establish collaborative relationships among triad • Communicate expectations and provide ongoing support to cooperating and student teachers • Complete observations of student teacher and provide feedback • Assess student teacher performance informally and formally
HLP Connection	• Understand, discuss, and explicitly model implementation of HLPs in the inclusive classroom • Provide ongoing feedback on student teacher's progress with implementation of HLPs	• Review HLPs with the cooperating and student teacher to ensure understanding • Provide resources to assist cooperating teacher with modeling of HLPs • Provide ongoing feedback on student teacher's progress with implementation of HLPs

Although the cooperating teacher and university supervisor are most directly connected, there are a number of additional people who influence the student teaching experience. Often, student teachers participate in an accompanying seminar course. This provides an opportunity for student teachers to build relationships with peers and teacher preparation faculty. Sharing placement experiences with peers can provide both professional and emotional support. A strong cohort helps student teachers

TABLE 1.3 Research on Effective Student Teacher Support

	What Does the Research Say?
Research Study	Key Takeaway
Lafferty, 2018	When cooperating teachers received formal and explicit training in how to effectively enact their role, student teachers perceived improvements in the quality of their field experiences. The findings suggest that professional development for cooperating teachers may increase the quality of field experiences for student teachers.
Boyd et al., 2009	Research has found that frequent observations by the university supervisor (at least 5), followed by a post-observation meeting and written feedback on specific competencies, benefits student teacher performance.

to recognize the value in collaboration, which will be a strength moving into the early career. This is particularly important for those who teach in inclusive environments and support students with a range of diverse needs.

School personnel can also contribute to a quality student teaching experience. Administrators, related service providers, team teachers, paraprofessionals, office staff, custodians, bus drivers, and food service employees all have an important role to play in the day-to-day functioning of the school. We encourage student teachers to introduce themselves to school staff and be involved in school-related events. This connection will broaden their support network and deepen their understanding of the community. Cooperating teachers can facilitate interactions between school staff and student teachers, creating opportunities for the student teacher to be involved. Table 1.3 shares some of the research on effective student teacher support.

Getting the Most Out of Student Teaching

Becoming a Reflective Practitioner

Throughout the book, we will offer reflection activities focused on specific elements of developing and implementing HLPs in an inclusive student teaching classroom. While reflection can be done formally, through activities and discussions with your cooperating teacher and university supervisor, we encourage student teachers to develop an informal, ongoing reflective practice. Set aside quiet time to think about the day, perhaps on your drive home from school, and consider keeping a journal.

Developing Resilience: Learning from Challenges

There is no perfect student teaching experience; expect that you will face challenges both in and out of the classroom. This is your opportunity to develop your skills and practice so that you are best prepared for your first year of teaching on your own. There will inevitably be lessons and interactions that don't go as well as you had hoped. That's OK! Let go of self-criticism and instead focus on self-reflection. How can you use every experience to improve the next?

Keeping Yourself Afloat

Teaching in the inclusive classroom, while rewarding, can also be emotionally challenging. Managing various preparation and instructional tasks can feel overwhelming. In addition to working to fulfill the requirements of a teacher preparation program and the expectations of a cooperating teacher and university supervisor, student teachers often strive to meet their own high expectations for their teaching performance. And, student teaching doesn't happen "in a bubble"; day-to-day responsibilities outside their placement still exist. Cooperating teachers and university supervisors can help student teachers stay afloat by clearly communicating expectations and providing extra support and flexibility when needed.

Self-Awareness and Stress Management during Student Teaching

We want to begin the conversation about self-awareness and stress management during student teaching with a discussion about work environments. While providing strategies for managing stress and maintaining mental health and well-being throughout the semester is important, ensuring that our student teachers are placed in healthy work environments is paramount. Toxic work environments do not provide the necessary

TABLE 1.4 Tips for Supporting Student Teacher SEL

CASEL Competency	Developing a Practice
Self-Awareness: "The abilities to understand one's own emotions, thoughts, and values and how they influence behavior across contexts."	Once a day, do a self-check-in. Make the self-check-in a habit by putting a reminder on your phone. During this time, identify your own emotions and reflect on how they may be affecting your performance in the classroom. Ask yourself: *How am I feeling right now? How are my feelings impacting my work?*
Self-Management: "The abilities to manage one's emotions, thoughts, and behaviors effectively in different situations and to achieve goals and aspirations."	Practicing mindfulness techniques can help you to regulate your emotions. Begin by observing, acknowledging, and labeling your feelings. Remind yourself that all feelings are OK and that you are not your feelings. Try to avoid blaming yourself or others. Ask yourself: *What strategies can I use to regulate my emotions so that I can act in a way that will help me to achieve my goals?*
Social Awareness: "The abilities to understand the perspectives of and empathize with others, including those from diverse backgrounds, cultures, and contexts."	Use strategies to build a positive classroom community. Get to know your students' family backgrounds and cultures. Share your perspectives and feelings with your students, and encourage them to share with you. Practice being non-judgmental and not personalizing others' behavior.
Relationship Skills: "The abilities to establish and maintain healthy and supportive relationships and to effectively navigate settings with diverse individuals and groups."	Practice active listening and reflect and validate others' feelings. Communicate your goals and don't be afraid to ask for help when you need it. Remember that relationships take time and require vulnerability. Ask yourself: *What small things can I do to build positive and supportive relationships with colleagues and students?*
Responsible Decision-Making: "The abilities to make caring and constructive choices about personal behavior and social interactions across diverse situations."	We make so many decisions in the classroom. At the end of the day, reflect on the choices you made and the interactions you had with colleagues and students. Ask yourself: *How have I demonstrated caring for myself and others through my actions and choices today?*

environment for student teachers to grow their professional practice. While student teachers will undoubtedly face stressful situations and perhaps experience some negative interactions, the university supervisor should monitor the health of the school and classroom environment and address concerns as they arise.

Even when placed in the most optimal environment, student teachers benefit from learning and practicing skills to enhance their self-awareness, manage stress, regulate emotions, and develop healthy work relationships. The Collaborative for Social Emotional Learning (CASEL.org) outlines five core competencies of Social Emotional Learning (SEL) in schools and classrooms, and we can encourage student teacher well-being by supporting their own development of SEL skills within each competency. Strengthening SEL skills is beneficial for children and adults, and the student teaching experience allows soon-to-be teachers to deepen their own skills in a supportive environment. Table 1.4 provides some ideas for how student teachers can develop their own practice. It is important for mentors to support this process; student teacher SEL development can and should be encouraged by both the cooperating teacher and the university supervisor. Mentors can do this by modeling practices throughout the day and setting aside time during meetings to check in with student teachers about their practice. Table 1.5 offers insight into some of the research connected to teacher well-being.

TABLE 1.5 Research on Teacher Well-Being

	What Does the Research Say?
Research Study	*Key Takeaway*
Greenberg et al., 2016	Teaching is a high-stress profession. Effective interventions to support teacher well-being and improve outcomes for teachers and students include SEL programming, mindfulness, and mentoring.
Corcoran & O'Flaherty, 2022	Given significant decreases in several sub-domains of psychological well-being during four-year programming, evidence-based teacher preparation is needed to support pre-service teachers' social and emotional well-being.

Perspectives in Practice: Raven's First Day

First days can be daunting, and there may be a lot running through your head. *What if the students see me as an outsider? Will I have good chemistry with my mentor teacher? What are all the classroom procedures? How prepared am I, really?*

If you feel these things on your first day of student teaching, know that you're not alone. Others have been there before, and these emotions are valid. No matter your level of excitement or enthusiasm, the start of student teaching can be overwhelming at times. For the first time, you are thrust into a real classroom setting—one with its own unique dynamic, routines, and set of student personalities.

Raven, a full-time student teacher in a 4th-grade classroom with no prior classroom experience, started her first day with all those emotions and more. "I definitely was really nervous," Raven noted. What helped guide Raven through her first day was thinking about her students. "I am there to learn to help students in the future," she remarked, "and the best way for me to do that is to not be nervous and think about the process."

However, this can be difficult to acknowledge in the moment, and Raven recognized that shifting your mindset doesn't happen overnight. The nervous jitters can still come up, but Raven takes the time to calm her nerves by reminding herself of the long-term opportunity this provides her to impact students in the future. It's just one step at a time.

Regardless of your level of first-day nerves, it may be difficult to know where to start when setting yourself up for a successful semester. Some pieces of advice from current student teachers include:

- Remind yourself that you have prepared for this moment: You are ready and the time is now.
- Don't be afraid to jump in from the start: Some mistakes are inevitable, and you will learn from them.
- It's okay to feel confused at first: Take a deep breath and know that your cooperating teacher and supervisor have your back.

Don't doubt yourself! Your experiences will enrich not only yourself, but the teachers, students, and school community around you. This is the start of an exciting new chapter that will help you become the best teacher you can be.

Mentorship Corner: Getting Off to a Good Start

Tips for Cooperating Teachers

- The first few weeks of school are especially important for setting teaching expectations and for establishing a positive, productive, and inclusive learning environment. If your student teacher is present at the beginning of the new school year, involve them in teaching and reinforcing expectations. If your student teacher is joining you later in the year, ask the students to share classroom expectations with them, and be sure to communicate how students learned expectations at the start of the year.
- Share your strategies for organizing lesson plans and daily activities. Although your student teacher may develop their own organizational strategies, it is important for them to understand how the class is organized.
- Introduce your student teacher to members of the school community and familiarize them with school procedures.
- Share information about students. What are the specific needs in your class? Which students have IEPs and 504 plans? Be sure to review any related paperwork necessary for the student teacher to meet your students' needs.
- Related services: Typically, the student teacher spends time observing you teach at the start of their placement. Consider arranging for your student teacher to observe other teachers, such as the special education teacher or ESL teacher, and related service providers.

Tips for University Supervisors

- Provide formal and explicit preparation for the cooperating teacher prior to the start of the semester. This meeting should include a review of all program-specific

expectations and the cooperating teacher's responsibilities. It is also important to familiarize the coordinating teacher with HLPs. Share HLP resources and videos. Discuss the importance of explicitly modeling HLP practices and explore scaffolding ideas for supporting student teachers as they learn to implement HLPs. Develop a plan for observing student teachers that includes collecting quantitative and qualitative data on HLPs and providing specific performance feedback on progress.
- ◆ Establish well-functioning triads: Work to establish a three-way rapport between you, the cooperating teacher, and the student teacher. See our guidance for an effective initial triad meeting in Appendix A.
- ◆ Create and share a "Student Teaching Newsletter" to introduce yourself and provide helpful guidance for getting started.

Practice and Reflect: Application Activities to Support Your Development

In Your Classroom

- Student teacher: Identify your goals for the semester. Talk with your cooperating teacher about your goals to get feedback and to see if they are reasonable. Determine, with your cooperating teacher, how you can begin to take steps toward meeting your goals.

In Seminar or Post-observation Meetings

- University supervisor: Establish a "check-in check-out" routine as part of your weekly seminar. Student teachers can use the time to reflect on the week, share experiences with their peers, make connections to HLPs, and identify goals for the upcoming weeks. Use this time to support student teacher SEL development by asking related reflection questions.

On Your Own

- Prepare ahead to minimize stress throughout the semester. Develop organization systems, review and ask questions about your program's expectations, consider how you will maintain healthy habits, and identify a support system.

Teacher Toolbox: Resources for Further Exploration

1. High Leverage Practices for Inclusive Classrooms (highleveragepractices.org)[1]: We will refer to this webpage in the following chapters and make connections to specific videos in application activities. To get started, check out the website and familiarize yourself with the HLPs in the Build Knowledge[2] section.
2. The Collaborative for Academic, Social, and Emotional Learning (CASEL.org)[3]: In Chapter 3, "The Classroom Environment," we will examine SEL practices in the classroom. Student teachers can begin to think about their own social-emotional health by exploring the fundamentals of SEL[4] on the CASEL webpage.
3. Consider registering on the site Capturing Observations and Collaboratively Sharing Educational Data (COACHED).[5] This video platform is designed to assist university supervisors by offering customizable feedback based on observational data.

Notes

1. https://highleveragepractices.org/
2. https://highleveragepractices.org/search?query=%20&f%5B0%5D=i_want_to%3A240&f%5B1%5D=i_want_to%3A240
3. https://casel.org/
4. https://casel.org/fundamentals-of-sel/
5. https://coachedweb.azurewebsites.net/

References

Boyd, D., Grossman, P., Lankford, H., Loeb, S., & Wyckoff, J. (December 2009). Teacher preparation and student achievement. *Educational Evaluation and Policy Analysis, 31*, 416–440.

Corcoran, R. P., & O'Flaherty, J. (2022). Social and emotional learning in teacher preparation: Pre-service teacher well-being. *Teaching and Teacher Education, 110*, 103563.

Greenberg, M. T., Brown, J. L., & Abenavoli, R. M. (2016). *Teacher stress and health effects on teachers, students, and schools*. Edna Bennett Pierce Prevention Research Center, Pennsylvania State University, 1–12.

Lafferty, K. E. (2018). The difference explicit preparation makes in cooperating teacher practice. *Teacher Education Quarterly, 45*(3), 73–95.

McFarland, J., Hussar, B., Zhang, J., Wang, X., Wang, K., Hein, S., Diliberti, M., Forrest Cataldi, E., Bullock Mann, F., & Barmer, A. (2019). *The condition of education 2019* (NCES 2019-144). U.S. Department of Education. National Center for Education Statistics. Retrieved [date] from https://nces.ed.gov/use-work/resource-library/report/compendium/condition-education-2019.

McLeskey, J., Billingsley, B., Brownell, M. T., Maheady, L., & Lewis, T. J. (2019). What are high-leverage practices for special education teachers and why are they important? *Remedial and Special Education, 40*(6), 331–337.

Rodriguez, J. A., & Murawski, W. W. (2020). *Special education law and policy: From foundation to application*. Plural Publishing.

APPENDIX A: INTRODUCTORY TRIAD MEETING

Pre-meeting considerations:

- Prior to the meeting, provide your cooperating and student teachers with written materials outlining each person's responsibilities and requirements for the semester.
- Provide your cooperating and student teachers with HLP resources so they can be reviewed prior to meeting.
- Plan the goals and structure of the meeting.
- Plan time for addressing questions/concerns.

During meeting considerations:

- Be sure to articulate the goals and structure of the meeting and to allow time for questions.
- Work to establish positive and collaborative three-way rapport between the university supervisor, the cooperating teacher, and the student teacher.

- Review all state and teacher prep program-level expectations for student teaching.
- Review HLPs that support an inclusive classroom.
- Discuss strategies for explicitly modeling specific teaching practices (HLPs) that best support diverse classrooms, including appropriate instruction and supports for students with disabilities.
- Discuss strategies for successful observations, including pre- and post-observation meetings, as well as strategies for scaffolding support and for implementing HLPs.

Post-meeting considerations:

- Email a brief follow-up summary of the meeting, being sure to encourage ongoing communication and collaboration.

2

The Inclusive Classroom

Dorian is an undergraduate pre-service teacher majoring in early childhood and elementary education, and he has been looking forward to beginning his student teaching in a local second-grade classroom. He recently spoke to his cooperating teacher to learn more about the school and the students in the class. He learned that there is a diverse range of strengths and abilities in the class of 18 students. Two students in the class already have Individualized Education Programs (IEPs). The cooperating teacher explained that one additional student is being evaluated for special education and that she is providing intervention for two additional struggling students who are behind their peers to determine if a referral for evaluation is necessary. Dorian is so excited to get started and meet his class. Still, he is feeling a bit anxious and wonders if he is fully prepared to support each and all of the students so that they can grow academically and socially.

If Dorian's scenario sounds relatable, rest assured that you are not alone in feeling a range of emotions as you prepare for your semester. In fact, many novice teachers report feeling inadequately prepared to teach in inclusive classrooms (Loreman et al., 2013). While potentially overwhelming at times, student teaching in the inclusive classroom can provide you with a solid foundation for supporting a wide range of students in your early career classroom. In this chapter, we provide an overview of special education law and outline the range of possible student-teacher experiences, all of which will lead to increased preparedness. We want to note that this chapter does not provide

DOI: 10.4324/9781003426738-3

a comprehensive overview of special education and is best used as a review following an Introduction to Special Education course. Student teachers who could not complete an introductory course before student teaching may benefit from the "Tools for Further Exploration" section at the end of this chapter. In the meantime, don't be afraid to ask many questions this semester; we encourage you to use this time to learn as much as you can about your responsibilities as a general education teacher and about how to implement effective inclusive practices so that you are well-prepared for your first inclusive classroom.

Looking Back: A Brief History of the Inclusive Classroom

Let's step back in time and consider the experiences of students with disabilities before the 1975 enactment of the Education of Handicapped Children Act (PL 94-142), which today is known as the Individuals with Disabilities Education Act (IDEA, 2004), and the 1990 passage of the Americans with Disabilities Act (ADA). Before 1975, the majority of students with disabilities did not have access to public education, and those who were able to attend public schools did not have IEPs to support their progress and meet their educational needs (U.S. Department of Education, n.d.). Some states had laws designed to exclude students with disabilities from receiving an education, and many students with disabilities were ultimately institutionalized, left to live in inhumane and abusive conditions (U.S. Department of Education, n.d.). Whether at home or at school, most students with disabilities were without opportunities to learn and were left to struggle.

The passage of the ADA and PL 94-142 resulted in numerous positive changes for students with disabilities. Eligible students with disabilities now have access to 504 plans and IEPs. The majority of students receiving special education services (65%) spend the majority of their time in general education classrooms learning alongside non-disabled peers, and this has benefits for both groups of students (Hehir et al., 2016). Table 2.1 highlights some of the research on the positive effects of inclusive classrooms.

TABLE 2.1 Research on Outcomes of Inclusive Education

	What Does the Research Say?
Research Study	Key Takeaway
Kefallinou et al. (2020)	Inclusive education, which includes implementing evidence-based practices to support diverse student learners, has both academic and social benefits for students with disabilities.
Molina Roldan et al. (2021)	In this qualitative research study, researchers investigated outcomes of inclusive classrooms on non-disabled students and found that such students were more accepting of differences and experienced satisfaction when helping others to learn.
Jordan et al. (2009)	Teachers who view students with disabilities as their responsibility tend to use more effective teaching practices, leading to increased effectiveness for all students.

Schools in the United States are now providing special education services to over 7.5 million students (NCES, n.d.). This has increased graduation rates and improved post-secondary opportunities for people with disabilities (Goodman et al., 2014).

These positive steps toward more inclusive schools for students with disabilities have required that general education teachers understand their legal responsibilities and strengthen their implementation of practices to support their students who receive special education and/or related services. Student teaching allows you to develop your instructional practices to support all students while also receiving guidance from your cooperating teacher and university supervisor. All three triad members must recognize the value of this experience and work collaboratively to ensure their understanding of the special education process.

What's Needed for Successful Inclusion?

The responsibility of creating an inclusive environment where students with disabilities have access to the general education curriculum and are appropriately supported by special education services should be shared among many stakeholders.

Simply placing a student with a disability in a general education classroom without the appropriate supports in place is not inclusion; in fact, an unsupported placement can create numerous barriers to learning for all students and can lead to a challenging work environment for teachers. While we recognize that student teachers do not have control over some specific structural and school-wide factors that support inclusion, we want to increase your awareness of what is needed so that you are prepared to advocate for your students in the future.

While the passage of the ADA and PL 94-142 started a decades-long improvement in policies to support people with disabilities and expanded access to special education services, schools need adequate funding to carry out the IDEA provisions. Providing a free appropriate public education (FAPE) can be costly to school districts; however, even though the federal government agreed to fund 40% of the law, it actually only funds approximately 15% of IDEA. Leaving states and school districts to fund the gap left by the federal government, resulting in many under-resourced schools struggling to support their students who receive special education services.

In addition to needing both federal and state-level laws and funds to support successful inclusion, school districts must create school-wide policies that appropriately support teachers and students. School leaders can support inclusion in numerous ways. Recognizing and working to create a positive school culture with mutual respect between administrators and teachers can build the trust necessary for effective collaboration. School leaders can also protect planning and collaboration time, essential for implementing effective instructional practices to support all students. School leaders can commit to high-quality professional development for teachers in inclusive practice. Finally, research has shown that school leaders who overemphasize the importance of high-stakes testing outcomes may inadvertently interfere with the implementation of quality instruction (Hoppey & McLeskey, 2013). Instead, school leaders should use data to determine the optimal instructional choices.

Understanding what is needed from those outside the classroom, including policymakers and school leaders, can help

TABLE 2.2 Effective Inclusive Classroom Practices and Frameworks

Explicit Instruction	An evidence-based practice for designing and delivering effective and engaging lessons in a clear and concise manner; a systematic and direct approach that incorporates modeling, high student engagement, scaffolding, practice, and feedback (Archer & Hughes, 2010).
Differentiated Instruction	A teaching practice that involves differentiating both the classroom environment and one's teaching methods by making strategic adjustments to the content, the process, and/or the product in order to accommodate a diverse range of students in the inclusive classroom (Tomlinson, 2014).
Universal Design for Learning	A framework for optimizing teaching and learning by providing meaningful and multiple ways for students to access, engage, comprehend, and express learning (CAST, n.d.).
MTSS	A prevention-focused framework for providing effective, high-quality instruction and using data-based decisions to provide appropriate evidence-based intervention across academic, social, emotional, and behavioral domains (PaTTAN.net, n.d.).

teachers advocate for appropriate support for themselves and their students. With structural and school-wide support in place, teachers can more effectively create an inclusive learning environment that meets the needs of all students. Implementing evidence-based instructional practices and utilizing research-based frameworks to provide necessary interventions and support are essential to the inclusive classroom. Table 2.2 provides an overview of these practices and frameworks; we elaborate on these in the following chapters.

Key Takeaways

- *Since PL 94-142 (now IDEA) was passed in 1975, public schools are required to provide a free and appropriate education for all eligible students identified as having a disability and in need of special education services.*
- *The majority of students who receive special education services spend most of their day in the general education classroom. General education teachers need structural and school-wide support to create effective inclusive learning environments.*

♦ *Evidence-based instructional practices and frameworks such as explicit instruction, differentiated instruction, universal design for learning, and multi-tiered systems of support can help all students to make progress in inclusive classrooms, including those with disabilities.*

Getting to Know Special Education Law

The Individuals with Disabilities Education Act outlines eight core principles to support students with disabilities, and it is important that general education teachers are familiar with these principles (Bateman & Cline, 2016). Following Table 2.3, which provides a brief overview of each core principle, we provide greater detail about the IEP, including the IEP team, and how to implement an IEP in an inclusive classroom.

IEP Basics for Student Teachers

Who's Who on the IEP Team?

We hope you can attend an IEP meeting during your student teaching semester (see our preparation recommendations below). Hence, it is helpful to understand who will be present and what role they play at the meeting. Typically, a parent or guardian is invited to attend the meeting. If the student is over 16, they are also invited to attend. Sometimes, younger students may attend part of the meeting. Additionally, you can expect to see the special education teacher, a local agency representative (i.e., principal or special education director), a school psychologist or other professional who can interpret evaluation results, and a general education teacher. Depending on the student's needs, related service providers may also be in attendance (i.e., physical therapist, speech language pathologist).

Each team member can offer unique insight into a student's academic, social, emotional, and behavioral strengths and needs. For example, a parent can describe the child's functioning and

TABLE 2.3 Core Principles of IDEA (Bateman & Cline, 2016)

Free Appropriate Public Education (FAPE)	Special education services are required by law to be provided at no cost to families. The education should be appropriate and demonstrate progress in the general education curriculum.
Nondiscriminatory Evaluation	As part of the disability identification process, students must receive an evaluation conducted by a trained professional. All suspected areas of disability should be assessed, and testing should be conducted in the student's native language. Eligibility decisions must be made by a team.
The Individualized Education Program (IEP)	All students eligible for special education services should receive an IEP, which is essentially a contract between the school district and family.
Least Restrictive Environment (LRE)	LRE determines where an eligible child should receive special education services. For many students with disabilities, the general education classroom is the least restrictive setting, and they should only be moved to a more restrictive setting after methods have been tried and not been successful.
Parent and Student Participation/ Due Process	Parents must provide consent to evaluate their child, and be considered an equal part of the IEP process. They must agree to any changes in their child's program or placement.
Confidentiality	Information about students with disabilities should be shared only on a need-to-know basis.
Zero Reject/Child Find	School districts are responsible for seeking out and identifying any child with a disability that lives within their jurisdictions.
Related Services	These services help students with disabilities benefit from special education. Examples of related services are speech and language, occupational therapy, social work, and transportation services.

circumstances outside the school day, while a special education teacher brings expertise regarding instructional strategies and supports. As a future general education teacher, you will have unique insight into the student's performance in the general education curriculum and inclusive classroom setting. You can speak to how this student compares to peers in terms of both academic and social, emotional, and behavioral performance, how they interact with peers, and the interventions and supports you have utilized as part of the prereferral process.

The Process: Pre-referral, Referral, and Evaluation

Only a small percentage of students who receive special education services are identified in early childhood before attending Kindergarten. Often, it is the general education teacher who first notices that a student is behind peers and having difficulty in the classroom. However, many factors may lead to a student being behind peers; this does not mean that the child necessarily has a disability and requires special education services. For this reason, it is essential to take steps in the classroom before making a referral for an evaluation for special education. A lot can be done in the general education classroom to support struggling students, and gaps can be closed through classroom-based interventions without the need for special education. Intervention and the use of specific instruction strategies in the general education classroom help distinguish students who can be successful in general education from those in need of special education. The following chapters review social, emotional, behavioral, and academic practices to support students effectively in general education settings. If these practices and frameworks (i.e., differentiated instruction and multi-tiered systems of support [MTSS]) have been solidly implemented with little success, we can be more confident in referring a student for an evaluation.

When a general education teacher refers a student for an evaluation, or when a parent makes an evaluation request, a multidisciplinary team obtains parental permission and then begins the evaluation. As the general education teacher, you can provide the team with student work samples, the interventions already implemented to support the student, and data that reflect the student's current performance. The multidisciplinary team will conduct the evaluation and eventually determine eligibility for services. You are an essential part of this entire process.

What Happens Next?

Once the evaluation is complete, the multidisciplinary team will meet to determine if the student qualifies for special education services. There are several reasons why a student may not be eligible for services; for example, the student's performance could improve due to interventions provided through MTSS. Students who qualify for special education services will do so under one or more of the 13 disability categories outlined in IDEA. These include high-incidence disabilities such as specific learning disabilities and speech and language disorders, and low-incidence disabilities such as multiple disabilities and autism spectrum disorder. Once the team makes a determination that the student is eligible for special education services, the IEP team (formerly the multidisciplinary team) will work together to develop the IEP, a program designed specifically for the student that outlines goals, services, placement, supplementary aids and services, supports for the general education teacher, and a plan for monitoring performance and participating in state assessments. If the student is over 16, a plan for postsecondary transition is also included in the IEP.

What to Expect at an IEP Meeting

Following introductions and a review of procedural safeguards, IEP meetings follow a process that typically mirrors the sequence of the IEP document. As the general education teacher, your cooperating teacher has a very important role at this meeting. They will share information regarding the student's present levels of performance, and this information is crucial for developing relevant goals and objectives, determining necessary accommodations and modifications, and making decisions about the most appropriate placement. As a student teacher, you and your cooperating teacher can work together to determine what your role should be at any IEP meetings you are able to attend. Table 2.4 offers suggestions for how you can prepare for your first IEP meeting, and Table 2.5 provides a list of common

TABLE 2.4 IEP Meeting: Preparation Checklist

- Be prepared! Plan out what you will share, review any relevant paperwork prior to the meeting, and understand the process and what to expect. Bring data and work samples to share with team members.
- Be professional! Introduce yourself to the team and the family, be on time, and keep cell phones and other distractions out of sight. Avoid diagnosing a child and/or recommending medication. For example, do not say: "Your son appears to have ADHD. Have you tried Ritalin?" Instead, point to the child's specific concerning behaviors.
- Be respectful! Actively listen to all team members, especially family members. Maintain confidentiality of all students. Avoid using jargon, which may be perceived as unwelcoming to families.

TABLE 2.5 Special Education Common Acronyms

Term	What is it?
AT	Assistive Technology: Any device or piece of equipment that is used to maintain or improve the functional capabilities of a student with a disability (e.g., pencil grip or communication system).
BASC	Behavior Assessment System for Children: An instrument used to measure and monitor the behavioral and/or social capabilities of a child.
BCBA	Board Certified Behavior Analyst: A professional who assesses and develops behavior treatment plans for students with behavioral challenges.
BIP/PSP	Behavior Intervention Plan or Positive Support Plan: An individual plan developed to support a student's progress toward behavioral and social IEP goals.
ESY	Extended School Year: Students with unique needs may require services beyond the academic school year.
FBA	Functional Behavior Assessment: A process for determining the function (the why?) behind a student's behavior. This is most often conducted by a behavior specialist or BCBA.
LEA	Local Education Agency: This refers to the school district and is often represented by a district administrator
MTSS	Multi-Tiered System of Support: A framework that provides varying levels of academic, behavioral, and social support based on student needs. School teams use data-based decision-making and evidence-based interventions across tiers, increasing intensity when needed.
OT	Occupational Therapy: This related service supports students who have fine motor skills needs.
PLOP/ PLAAFP	Present Levels of Performance or Academic Achievement Functional Performance: This section of the IEP provides a picture of the student's current abilities and progress in the general education curriculum.
PT	Physical Therapy: This related service supports students who have gross motor skills needs.
SDI	Specially Designed Instruction: Instruction that is individualized and developed with the intention of meeting IEP goals.
SLP	Speech and Language Pathologist: A professional who provides speech and language therapy to students with language-based needs.

acronyms used at IEP meetings. While this list is not exhaustive, it will help to familiarize you with those most commonly used. See the "Mentorship Corner" and "Practice and Reflect" sections for ideas about how your participation can be scaffolded so that you gradually gain confidence with this process.

Time to Implement! Putting the IEP into Practice

The IEP is a legal document that outlines a specific program for a student with a disability/ies. As we have already discussed, under IDEA, students with disabilities have both the right to be included with non-disabled peers as much as possible and the right to be placed in the least restrictive environment possible. Therefore, general education teachers must be very familiar with their students' IEPs; they have a responsibility to carry out specific accommodations and modifications, and to monitor individual progress goals, all while teaching in the general education classroom. This includes student teachers, who are responsible for delivering instruction and who are therefore responsible for making any necessary accommodations and modifications. Table 2.6 provides an overview of connections to HLPs throughout the remaining chapters that will assist with successful IEP implementation in the inclusive classroom.

Key Takeaways

- *School districts and teams must abide by the specific principles outlined in IDEA. Learning these principles will help general education teachers to understand the purpose and goals of the law.*
- *As a member of the multidisciplinary team, the general education teacher has a unique role to play throughout the pre-referral and referral.*
- *The IEP is a legal document, and general education teachers are responsible for contributing to the present levels of performance and development of goals, making appropriate accommodations and modifications outlined in the IEP, and monitoring student progress.*

TABLE 2.6 High Leverage Practice Connections

Collaboration HLPs	HLPs 1, 2, and 3 review effective collaboration practice with colleagues, professionals, and families that support student learning and help teams to access necessary services for eligible students.	Continue to learn about collaboration HLPs in Chapter 7. We provide strategies for working with professionals and families.
Assessment HLPs	HLPs 4, 5, and 6 review effective practices for gathering data, interpreting and communicating assessment results, and adjusting instruction based on assessment outcomes.	Continue to learn about assessment HLPs in Chapters 4 and 6. We provide strategies for assessing and monitoring progress in both behavioral and academic areas.
Social/ Emotional Behavioral HLPs	HLPs 7–10 review effective practices for supporting students' social, behavioral, and emotional skills including considerations for the classroom environment, use of feedback, teaching social skills, and implementing behavior support plans.	Continue to learn about SEB HLPs in Chapters 3 and 4. We provide strategies for creating an organized, nurturing environment to support student behavior.
Instruction HLPs	HLPs 11–23 review effective practices for instruction in the inclusive classroom including planning and delivering explicit instruction, actively engaging learners, and scaffolding support.	Continue to learn about instruction HLPs in Chapters 5 and 6. We provide strategies for scaffolding, providing feedback, and engaging all students.

Perspectives in Practice: A First-Year Teacher Prepares for a First IEP Meeting

Grace is a brand-new elementary school teacher in a 5th-grade inclusive classroom. She is preparing for her first IEP meeting for one of her students who is up for his annual review, and she is feeling grateful for the practice opportunities she had during her pre-service preparation. This included the chance to attend several IEP meetings alongside her cooperating teacher during her student teaching semester. She remembers feeling very anxious about talking to parents at IEP meetings but, as she gained more experience, her confidence increased. In preparation for her first IEP meeting as the general education team member, Grace reviews her notes from student teaching to help her create a to-do list:

- Gather and summarize relevant assessment and progress monitoring data.
- Summarize the general education curriculum so that all team members develop an understanding of overarching goals, content, activities, and expectations in the inclusive classroom.
- Gather student work samples to share at the IEP meeting.
- Be positive. Prepare to share strengths and observations of academic, social, and behavioral growth.
- Prepare to share challenges along with insights and ideas into how any concerns may be addressed.
- Avoid using educational jargon, which may make parents feel uncomfortable or unwelcome.

Mentorship Corner: Strengthening Understanding of the Special Education Process

Tips for Cooperating Teachers

- Ensure that your student teacher has access to all IEPs and 504 plans for their students this semester. Review these plans with your student teacher, paying close attention to the accommodations and modifications necessary to support students with disabilities in the general education classroom.
- Scaffold guidance and feedback for planning lessons that utilize instructional strategies that support all students. Share your rationale for using selected strategies and provide planning support and feedback as your student teacher assumes more responsibility in the classroom.
- Scaffold support for team meetings (multidisciplinary teams, IEP teams). As the semester progresses, encourage your student teacher to participate in these meetings.
- Discuss and share specific strategies for effective communication and collaboration with professionals in the

building who have a role in supporting students, such as special education teachers and related service providers.
- ♦ Help your student teacher to arrange an observation with related service providers who support your students.

Tips for University Supervisors
- ♦ Remember that each student teacher will have a very unique experience when it comes to providing special education services in their student teaching classroom. This is dependent on the make-up of the class and the structure of the school. Allow for a lot of discussion both in your meetings and in seminar, where students can learn from each other.
- ♦ Develop brief assignments to support your student teacher's understanding of the special education process and of how to support students with disabilities in the general education classroom. For example, a student teacher identifies one student for a "case study." As part of this assignment, the student teacher can review records, interview teachers, conduct research into characteristics of the selected student's disability, and "shadow" the student for a day.
- ♦ Provide individualized and specific feedback to plans and instruction during your post-observation meetings regarding support for special education students in the class.

Practice and Reflect: Application Activities to Support Your Development

In Your Classroom

- You will be responsible for teaching students with IEPs and 504 plans this semester, which means that you will have to plan for appropriate accommodations and modifications to your instruction. Familiarize yourself with your students' IEPS and 504 plans by reading through them carefully. Make a list of questions for your cooperating teacher. Participate in opportunities to collaborate with special education teachers and related service providers as often as possible.

(Cont.)

In Seminar or Post-observation Meetings
• Share your experiences with fellow student teachers. Remember that special education is individualized, so the experiences of cohort members are unique.
• Ask for feedback on your lesson plans and during post-observation meetings. Prior to an observation, share concerns about meeting the needs of all students in your inclusive class and ask your supervisor for feedback on specific areas you want to target for growth.

On Your Own
• Be patient with yourself as you learn the ins and outs of special education. Don't be afraid to ask a lot of questions.

Teacher Toolbox: Resources for Further Exploration

1. IRIS module on Developing High-Quality Individualized Education Programs:[1] Complete this module to review requirements for IEPs that are outlined in IDEA. This module also provides a detailed overview of the special education identification process.
2. IRIS module on The Prereferral Process: Procedures for Supporting Students with Academic and Behavioral Concerns.[2]
3. Understood Explains Podcast (Season 1)[3]: Understood.org is a nonprofit organization that provides resources and support for people with disabilities, their families, and the educational community. Season 1 of the Understood Explains podcast focuses on the process of special education identification.
4. Center for Parent Information and Resources: 10 Basic Steps in Special Education.[4] This resource provides information about the special education process for families and educators.

Notes

1. https://iris.peabody.vanderbilt.edu/module/iep01/#content
2. https://iris.peabody.vanderbilt.edu/module/preref/

3. https://www.understood.org/podcasts/understood-explains
4. https://www.parentcenterhub.org/steps/

References

Americans with Disabilities Act (1990). 42 U.S.C. § 12101 et seq.
Archer, A. L., & Hughes, C. A. (2010). *Explicit instruction: Effective and efficient teaching*. Guilford Publications.
Bateman, D. F., & Cline, J. L. (2016). *A teacher's guide to special education*. ASCD.
CAST. (n.d.). https://udlguidelines.cast.org/
Education for All Handicapped Children Act (1975). Pub. L. No. 94-142, 89 Stat. 773.
Goodman, J. I., Bucholz, J., Hazelkorn, M., & Duffy, M. L. (2014). Using graduation rates of students with disabilities as an indicator of successful inclusive education. In *Measuring inclusive education* (pp. 279–301). Emerald Group Publishing Limited. https://doi.org/10.1108/S1479-363620140000003030
Hehir, T., Grindal, T., Freeman, B., Lamoreau, R., Borquaye, Y., & Burke, S. (2016). A summary of the evidence on inclusive education. *Abt Associates*. https://files.eric.ed.gov/fulltext/ED596134.pdf
Hoppey, D., & McLeskey, J. (2013). A case study of principal leadership in an effective inclusive school. *The Journal of Special Education*, *46*(4), 245–256.
Individuals with Disabilities Education Act (2004). 20 U.S.C. § 1400 et seq..
Jordan, A., Schwartz, E., & McGhie-Richmond, D. (2009). Preparing teachers for inclusive classrooms. *Teaching and Teacher Education*, *25*(4), 535–542.
Kefallinou, A., Symeonidou, S., & Meijer, C. J. (2020). Understanding the value of inclusive education and its implementation: A review of the literature. *Prospects*, *49*(3-4), 135–152.
Loreman, T., Sharma, U., & Forlin, C. (2013). Do pre-service teachers feel ready to teach in inclusive classrooms? A four country study of teaching self-efficacy. *Australian Journal of Teacher Education (Online*, *38*(1), 27–44.
Molina Roldán, S., Marauri, J., Aubert, A., & Flecha, R. (2021). How inclusive interactive learning environments benefit students without special needs. *Frontiers in Psychology*, *12*, 661427.

National Center for Education Statistics (NCES) (n.d.). https://nces.ed.gov/programs/coe/indicator/cgg/students-with-disabilities

PaTTAN. (n.d.). https://www.pattan.net/Evidence-Based-Practices/Multi-Tiered-System-of-Support.

Tomlinson, C. A. (2014). *The differentiated classroom: Responding to the needs of all learners*. ASCD.

U.S. Department of Education (n.d.). www.ed.gov/idea/

3
The Classroom Environment

Ayden is three weeks into her student teaching experience. She has observed her cooperating teacher effectively deliver numerous lessons, has regularly conferenced with individual students, and has frequently conducted small group instruction; she is now ready to lead whole group math instruction. As soon as she begins the lesson, one student repeatedly calls out questions and responses. Then, a table of students starts whispering to and laughing with one another. Finally, when Ayden directs the class to practice math problems independently, one student gets up and walks to the corner of the room, and another puts her head down on her desk, both refusing to get started. Ayden feels disappointed, frustrated, and confused; she had prepared her lesson plan, she had all her materials ready, and she was excited to begin teaching her students. Her cooperating teacher rarely had any of these challenges. Ayden keeps asking herself, "What went wrong?"

Ask anyone who has been teaching for a while, and they will tell you that even the best lessons can go awry due to unexpected student behavior. Teachers who proactively, positively, and equitably support student behavior often do so by utilizing key practices that can be difficult to identify because they are embedded into the daily routines and language within the classroom. In this chapter, we will unearth those key practices, so you can begin to use them and develop a positive, predictable, and safe learning environment.

Why Positive, Predictable, Safe Learning Environments?

Think back to a grade or class where you were highly successful. What made you achieve in that environment? Most often, people say something like, "The teacher believed in me," "I knew what I was supposed to do," or "The teacher made the information interesting." It turns out these statements point to what research identifies as critical positive, proactive practices to support and respond to students' social-emotional-behavioral (SEB) development.

The term SEB provides a comprehensive term encompassing how people relate to others (social), feel (emotional), and act (behavioral) (Chafouleas, 2020). When students' SEB needs are adequately supported, they are more likely to experience increased instructional time due to fewer disruptions, higher rates of student engagement, and increased on-task behavior (e.g., Gage & MacSuga-Gage, 2017; Scott, 2016; Simonsen et al., 2008). This leads to a more equitable pathway toward academic achievement for students and their peers. Table 3.1 provides further examples of research studies pointing to the positive impacts of a preventative approach in the classroom.

Supporting students' SEB needs benefits educators, too! Feeling overwhelmed with student SEB needs is one of the top causes of stress and burnout for teachers (Herman et al., 2018).

TABLE 3.1 Research Highlighting Positive Impacts of a Preventative Approach

	What Does the Research Say?
Condliffe et al., 2022	This randomized control trial examined the effects of PBIS (MTSS-B) on student outcomes. Among students with the most behavioral needs, the study found Tier 1 support (prevention) is an integral component for their success.
Wills et al., 2023	In this study, teachers were trained to implement key classroom management practices (e.g., explicit teaching of behavior expectations, high rates of praise). Classrooms of trained teachers experienced higher rates of on-task student behavior for all and fewer disruptions from at-risk students than classrooms without trained teachers.

However, teachers who receive training and adequately support students' SEB needs experience improved perceptions of their classroom climate, feel more efficacious, and claim less stress (Reinke et al., 2013).

Background Considerations for SEB Support Practices

MTSS/PBIS Framework
Chapter 2 introduced the multi-tiered systems of support (MTSS) framework as a way to organize resources, provide instruction, and support the varying needs of students. Positive Behavioral Interventions and Supports (PBIS) is an MTSS framework emphasizing SEB supports along with academics. Ideally, schools develop a PBIS/MTSS framework throughout their entire school by identifying common school-wide behavior expectations that are explicitly taught, prompted, reinforced, and instructively corrected. Classroom teachers then align the expectations for their classroom with school-wide expectations. This promotes consistency, strengthens understanding, and promotes equitable experiences. When implemented with fidelity, 80% of students will adequately respond to this universal (Tier 1) level of support. The remaining 20% of students may need some targeted (Tier 2) or individualized (Tier 3) support to achieve academic and/or social competence. Those supports are delivered to students based on data-driven decision-making and are routinely progress monitored to determine if supports need to be intensified or faded. If you are student teaching in a school that has not embraced a whole-school approach, you can still apply the PBIS/MTSS framework within your classroom.

Cultural Responsiveness
Each day, teachers interact with a wide range of students from diverse home and community backgrounds. Each student brings a unique learning history comprised of prior experiences based on their race/ethnicity, gender identity, sexual preference, socioeconomic status, family norms, age, peer experiences, religious beliefs, spoken language, disability status, and other diverse

factors. As a result, teachers must strive to utilize key SEB support practices in a way that equitably embraces, respects, and values students' cultures and development. This is a critical understanding as we aim to establish positive, predictable, safe learning environments where all students experience a sense of belonging.

Establish a Positive, Predictable Learning Environment

Over several decades of research, a few key practices have consistently demonstrated positive impacts on students' academic and SEB achievement. Cultivating positive relationships, promoting predictability and structure, identifying and explicitly teaching common expectations, reinforcing students when they engage in contextually appropriate behavior, and providing instructional responses to behavior errors are practices used to provide a solid Tier 1 foundation in the classroom. Students who have experienced trauma or have mental health needs such as anxiety will also benefit from having a safe, structured, predictable, and welcoming learning environment. As we define and provide implementation guidance for each practice throughout this chapter, consider if these practices are already implemented in your student teaching classroom. If so, connect with your cooperating teacher and identify how you can also engage in these practices. If not, share these practices with your cooperating teacher and determine how you can incorporate them into the classroom as you take on more responsibilities.

Cultivate Positive Relationships

When students experience positive relationships with educators, they participate more, are more likely to experience enjoyment in school, and engage in fewer disruptive behaviors (Cook et al., 2018; Martin & Collie, 2019). Positive teacher-student relationships have been shown to have long-term positive and protective impacts on students (Longobardi et al., 2016; O'Connor et al., 2011). Additionally, positive relationships between teachers and their students support teacher well-being (Aldrup et al., 2018). Taking the time to foster positive relationships with students is a critical component of establishing a positive, proactive classroom.

Greet Students at the Door
One simple, low-intensity practice is greeting students positively as they enter the classroom. When teachers meet their student at the door, state their students' names, engage in brief personal check-ins, prompt a classroom expectation, and direct their students to an activity, students increase on-task behavior and decrease disruptive behavior (Cook et al., 2018). This practice takes a few minutes at the start of class but has a significant positive impact on classroom and student outcomes.

Practice Active Supervision
Educators can reduce conduct problems and promote relationship-building by consistently and actively supervising students. This practice involves continuously scanning, circulating, and positively interacting with students with both verbal (e.g., praise, greetings, questions) and non-verbal (e.g., smile, nods, high fives) interactions (Colvin et al., 1997; Gage et al., 2020). Not only does this practice provide opportunities for educators to monitor student behavior, but it also connects educators with their students informally, allowing them to learn about student interests, preferences, and backgrounds while cultivating positive relationships.

As a student teacher, developing positive relationships with your students can begin on the first day in the classroom. Start by introducing yourself, conversing with students during less structured times of the day (e.g., snack, recess, transitions), and greeting students as they enter the classroom. Actively supervise when students are engaged in independent or small group work and interact positively as you go! Developing positive teacher-student relationships is the foundation for all the following practices.

Promote Predictability and Structure
Educators can set students up for success by proactively establishing efficiency, organization, and accessibility. When

students can successfully navigate the learning environment, they are better able to perform routines effectively, maximize instructional time, and self-manage their behavior. There are many strategies to enhance structure and predictability in classrooms. In this section, we will discuss considerations for the physical environment, schedules, and routines.

Consider Classroom Design

The physical environment of the classroom should be organized, practical, and effectively designed for learning. As furniture (desks, shelves, tables, etc.) is placed, educators must consider where students walk to enter and exit the room, transition between spaces within the room, look during instruction, and access necessary instructional materials (Haydon et al., 2019). It is also important to match instructional needs to the physical environment. For example, if most instruction occurs on individual electronic devices, the educator might deliver instruction standing behind student desks so that screens can be monitored. If students often engage in small group activities, traffic flow patterns between parts of the room will need to be identified differently than they would be in a classroom where students do most of their work independently at their desks. To ensure active supervision, clear lines of vision between students and educators, regardless of where anyone may be in the room, are critical (Scott, 2016). Educators should also consider the accessibility needs of a diverse student population. The physical environment must accommodate individual accessibility needs (e.g., movement, vision, hearing disabilities) and enhance executive functioning skills (e.g., labeled supplies, space for materials, posted protocols). Lastly, limit visual supports to those that are necessary for instruction. Classrooms with abundant clutter and excessive visual stimulation can negatively impact students' attention and memory skills (Rodrigues & Pandeirada, 2018). Effectively designing the physical environment can not only enhance student learning, but it can also prevent disruptive behaviors from happening (Cheryan et al., 2014).

Follow a Predictable Schedule

A predictable classroom schedule allows students to adequately prepare for instructional blocks, activities, and tasks. Educators can strengthen predictability by posting and regularly reviewing a daily schedule. When pre-determined disruptions to the daily schedule inevitably occur, teachers can notify students of the change as part of the daily schedule review and provide frequent reminders to proactively reduce challenges that may develop as a result of a changed schedule.

Routines and Procedures

Teaching and encouraging explicit routines and procedures (e.g., entering and exiting the classroom, asking for help, using bathrooms) can increase instructional time and improve students' SEB skills. Educators should first identify the routines and procedures that will most likely be needed in their classrooms. Next, determine the specific steps required to complete the routine or procedure. Then, teach the routine or procedure to the students and provide multiple opportunities for practice and feedback. Critical routines and procedures will be specific to each classroom context. Below are examples of commonly used routines and procedures:

- Entering and exiting the classroom
- Asking for help
- Use of bathrooms
- Sharpening pencils
- Technology storage
- Turn and talks
- Attention signals
- Turning in assignments
- Finishing work early

Establishing well-taught, consistent routines and procedures fosters student independence, decreases disruptions, and promotes an efficient, predictable learning environment for students and educators alike.

As a student teacher, consider what supports predictability and structure in the classroom. Ask your mentor teacher about what informed the decisions made regarding the physical environment, how the daily schedule was determined, and which routines and protocols are most important to the classroom learning environment. Additionally, consider how you can enhance and utilize the existing predictability and structure as you begin to take on more teaching responsibility. If you find a need to adjust or add any components, discuss your thoughts with your cooperating teacher so plans can be made to integrate your ideas into the classroom.

> **Key Takeaways**
>
> ♦ *Providing structure and predictability within the learning environment is a proactive way to support student success.*
> ♦ *Consider what routines and procedures would be most beneficial to students and teach students how to do them with many practice opportunities.*

Identify, Teach, Prompt, and Reinforce Common Expectations

Rather than assuming that students know how to "do school," effective educators collaborate with their students to identify, teach, prompt, and reteach positively stated expectations for the classroom community. Doing so promotes a predictable, positive, and more equitable learning environment where all students can be successful.

Identify Common Expectations

Begin identifying common expectations by linking any schoolwide expectations into the classroom context. If the school promotes expectations such as "Responsibility, Safety, Respect," then consider what it will look and feel like to demonstrate those expectations within the classroom. If your school does not have common school-wide expectations, identify and ideally co-construct common expectations with your students. Keep expectations broad, comprehensive, positively stated, 3–5 in number, and contextually appropriate for your students.

Teach Explicitly

Once those expectations have been identified, educators can provide explicit instruction (Archer & Hughes, 2010) on demonstrating the expected behavior across the various classroom contexts. Educators teach new academic skills by introducing, modeling, and providing opportunities for guided practice. The same level of instruction should be applied to teaching SEB expectations and skills as students move through the phases of learning (acquisition, fluency, maintenance, and generalization; Haring et al., 1978). Rather than telling students to "Show Respect," educators can teach and model how to show respect as students enter the classroom, during group instruction, while collaborating with peers, throughout independent work, and as students exit the room. Once students have received explicit instruction on how to show respect, they can be provided opportunities to practice. This vital and stark difference from just assuming students already know how to show respect decreases gaps in prior experiences, promotes common understanding, and strengthens predictability within the learning environment.

Prompt and Reteach Frequently

Once expectations have been identified and explicitly taught, educators need to consistently pre-correct and prompt expected behavior before the behavior is expected to occur (Ennis et al., 2017). We cannot assume that just because the behavior was taught once, it will be consistently used. Students will need pre-corrects and prompts to demonstrate the expectation, especially during predictable times when errors may occur, such as during transitions or after-school breaks. For example, before students go into the hallway, the teacher can remind students to move safely, quietly, and responsibly. This will likely lead to less disruptive behavior in the hallway.

Just as some students may require additional support with new academic skills, undoubtedly, some students may need more prompting and reteaching than others. The key is to know what your students need and proactively provide strategic prompting or reteaching of expectations and SEB skills as needed. If many students demonstrate errors with an expectation or SEB skill, it is likely time to provide a booster lesson and reteach the expectation!

Reinforce the Use of Expectations

Educators play a critical role in student behavior. How educators respond to student behavior can impact whether or not the behavior will occur again (Cooper et al., 2020). Once you have identified, taught, prompted, and retaught your classroom expectations and expected SEB skills, you want to respond in a way that increases the chances of those behaviors happening regularly. There are several practices educators can use to reinforce expected behavior, including providing high rates of specific praise (Gage & MacSuga-Gage, 2017), delivering a higher number of positive interactions than corrections (Caldarella et al., 2020), and establishing varied, equitable acknowledgment systems to support all students (Simonsen et al., 2008).

Specific Praise

In numerous studies, specific praise has been identified as a key predictor of student behavior across contexts (e.g., Gage & MacSuga-Gage, 2017; Simonsen et al., 2017). Specific praise is a positive statement given after a student engages in contextually appropriate behavior that specifically informs the student what they did well. Examples of specific praise include: "That was hard, and you stuck with it. Well done!"; "You came into the room with a calm body and put your materials away. Nice job being responsible!"; and "Thank you for being respectful by raising your hand before sharing." Notice that in each of these statements, the educator identifies the skill or SEB skill that was demonstrated, whereas general statements such as "Good job" leave a student not knowing what behavior or skill was valued or what they should engage in again. Providing high rates of specific praise can lead to positive student outcomes and should be used widely and frequently within classroom settings.

Positive-to-Negative Interactions

Positive-to-negative interactions between educators and students fall into three broad categories (a) positive, (b) negative, and

(c) neutral. Positive interactions include general and specific praise and non-verbal gestures such as smiles, nods, thumbs up, etc. Negative interactions include general and specific verbal reprimands or gestures indicating disapproval, such as shaking the head "no," giving "teacher looks," etc. Neutral interactions include verbal and non-verbal directives, questions, and responses to questions. Frequently identified as a practice with low intensity but high impact, positive teacher/student interactions have been shown to have a direct relationship with student on-task behavior (Caldarella et al., 2020). Studies have shown that, as teachers increased their praise and decreased their reprimands, students stayed more attentive to their classwork (Caldarella et al., 2020; Cook et al., 2017). Teacher/student interaction has also been shown to have positive, long-term impacts. For example, when educators provide high levels of negative interactions in the fall, students are more likely to engage in disruptive behavior and dysregulation in the spring. However, if educators provide high rates of positive interactions in the fall, students are more likely to demonstrate prosocial behavior in the spring (Reinke et al., 2008). The exact ratio needed for positive and optimal effects remains unclear (Sabey et al., 2019). However, a 4:1 or 5:1 ratio is commonly used as a goal for most students. Students with emotional-behavioral disorders may need a ratio as high as 9:1 (Caldarella et al., 2020). Regardless of the exact ratio, it is well-established that increasing positive teacher/student interactions and decreasing negative interactions improves student outcomes (Caldarella et al., 2020; Cook et al., 2017). Table 3.2 elaborates on further research about the benefits of praise.

Acknowledgment Systems

Verbal praise is a highly effective, easy-to-use strategy to acknowledge students for using prosocial SEB skills successfully. It can also be beneficial to incorporate class-wide acknowledgment systems to (a) remind educators to deliver praise and (b) provide students with a tangible, concrete representation of acknowledgment. Acknowledgment systems should be based on student developmental levels and SEB needs, personal

TABLE 3.2 Research Highlighting the Benefits of Teacher Praise

	What Does the Research Say?
Caldarella et al., 2020	There is a direct relationship between educator praise rates and on-task student behavior. The more educators praise students, the more students engage in contextually appropriate behavior.
Caldarella et al., 2021	While reprimands may temporarily pause contextually inappropriate behavior, they do not decrease disruptive behavior or improve on-task behavior in the long term.
Reinke et al., 2013	The more educators use praise, the more self-efficacy they experience. Educators feel less effective and more exhausted as student disruptions increase, and their own use of harsh reprimands increases. In this study, educators who had more negative interactions than positive interactions were more likely to report emotional exhaustion.

preferences of the educator and students, and feasibility. Additionally, the developed acknowledgment system should provide variable acknowledgment rates—frequent, intermittent, and long-term.

Acknowledgments, such as specific verbal praise, should be abundantly and frequently delivered throughout each school day. Other forms of acknowledgment, such as tokens, tickets, and written notes, should be provided intermittently with specific praise connected to any tangible item. Reinforcement provided intermittently can be used to provide access to long-term acknowledgment. Table 3.3 explains two common types of acknowledgment systems and provides an example of each.

Systems such as a group contingency or a token economy can provide a continuous delivery of acknowledgment. For example, Ms. Lank provides a high rate of verbal specific praise throughout the day (Frequent). Additionally, she occasionally pairs verbal praise with a chip to individual students to strengthen the acknowledgment. She aims to give out 25 chips each day (Intermittent). When students receive chips, they add them to a shared bucket. When the class collectively earns 500 chips, they can watch a movie together (Long-term).

TABLE 3.3 Types of Acknowledgement Systems

Acknowledgment System	What Is It?	Example
Group Contingency	Students gain access to a positive outcome when they engage in clearly identified behaviors. Group contingencies can be focused on the whole class, small groups, or individual students.	For every 5 minutes that Mr. Graves's class completes independent reading time without disruption, the class earns a star. When 10 stars are received, the class earns a preferred activity (recess, free time, movie, etc.).
Token Economy	Individual students earn points, tickets, or tallies toward rewards such as a preferred activity, homework pass, or tangible item for engaging in contextually appropriate behaviors.	Ms. Rodriguez prints out classroom "Bucks" that she gives to students when they are being prepared, respectful, and safe in the classroom. Students store their earned "Bucks" and have an opportunity to cash them in each Friday afternoon for extra iPad time, homework passes, or lunch in the classroom.

Key Takeaways

- *Identify, teach, prompt, and reinforce SEB expectations and skills as intentionally as you would a new academic skill.*
- *Acknowledge and reinforce students often for engaging in the SEB expectations and skills you have identified, taught, and prompted!*

Respond Instructionally to Behavior Errors

When strong Tier 1 SEB classroom practices are in place, we are proactively supporting our students while simultaneously preventing problems. Nonetheless, our students will still make mistakes from time to time. When behavior errors happen, teachers should consider a response that does little to interfere with classroom activities and uses an instructional approach.

Additionally, educators should aim to use a least to most intensity approach. Table 3.4 offers some common and effective strategies for responding to behavior errors:

TABLE 3.4 Strategies for Responding to SEB Errors

Strategy	What Is It?	Example
Proximity	The teacher reduces the space between herself and a student as a way to redirect and address behavior mistakes.	Ms. Butler observes that a student is off-task and disrupts classmates. She moves closer to the student without interrupting the lesson. The student stops the problem behavior and begins to work on the task.
Praise Appropriate Behavior in Others	As an alternative to correcting a student's behavior, a teacher provides behavior-specific praise to a different student who is displaying an alternative, appropriate behavior.	Rather than correcting a student for incorrectly putting away materials, Mr. Crosby thanked several students who put away materials correctly. The student fixes their materials.
Error Correction/ Redirection	In a quick, calm manner, the teacher provides specific feedback that alerts a student to stop undesired behavior and to engage in desired behavior.	A student is calling out. Ms. Hunter calmly asks the student to stop calling out and to raise their hand instead. The student does so.
Precision Request	A teacher makes a request for a student to engage in appropriate behavior using "please." After waiting five seconds with no response, the teacher asks again, using the word "need." The teacher delivers specific praise or an error correction depending on student response.	Mr. Melgar asks a student to please put his phone away. He waits five seconds, and the student is still using their phone. He tells the student he needs them to put their phone away. The student complies. Mr. Melgar provides specific praise.
Reteaching Expected Behavior	Refer to the classroom expectations. State the expectation that needs reteaching. Ask students to model the appropriate behavior. Follow up with prompting and specific feedback.	Ms. Ortiz notices that students are not following expectations when walking in the hallway. While referring to her classroom expectation matrix, she reminds them of the behavior. She asks a

TABLE 3.4 (Cont.)

Strategy	What Is It?	Example
		student to model what walking in the hallway should "look and sound like." She prompts students to meet this expectation the next several times they walk in the hallway and follows up with specific feedback.

Considerations for Responding to SEB Errors

Just as educators play a critical, proactive role in ensuring that students demonstrate appropriate SEB values and skills, they play an equally vital role in responding to SEB errors. Indeed, the way an educator responds to an SEB error can impact whether or not an error is repeated. For example, imagine Chris is a student struggling with a new math concept. When Chris's teacher asks the class to practice this new concept independently, Chris pushes the assignment away and puts their head down on the desk. The teacher must now decide how to respond. If the teacher sends Chris to the office, for example, and doesn't ask them to complete the assignment, Chris's SEB error winds up rewarding them because they avoid doing the challenging task. Chris's behavior has now been reinforced and will therefore likely occur again the next time they are asked to complete a challenging task. Before sending Chris to the office, then, Chris's teacher should consider whether or not Chris has the skills necessary to complete the task and then offer support accordingly. It is important to remember that each time a student makes an SEB error, there are many factors to take into consideration before making a response.

When SEB errors occur, educators need to consider the student's purpose, skills, and needs. Additionally, the educator should reflect upon how well the key positive, proactive Tier 1 practices described in this chapter have been delivered to the students. Consider the following questions as you respond to student SEB errors:

- Have I identified, taught, prompted, and reinforced the SEB expectations and skills needed for our learning environment effectively?
- Am I tired, hungry, stressed, etc.? If so, how is that impacting my response?
- Have I responded to the error calmly and privately?
- Have I considered whether or not a cultural difference has led to the error?
- What is the least intensive way to respond to the error?
- Does my response to the error match the severity of the error?
- Is this a repeated error that is serving a purpose for the student? If so, what is the student trying to obtain or avoid?
- Does the student need support in certain skills?

Responding to SEB errors is complex and needs to be done intentionally. Educators should aim to decrease the likelihood of repeated errors occurring by considering how they respond, individual student needs, and the strength of their key Tier 1 practices. As a student teacher, be sure to ask your cooperating teacher how SEB errors are addressed in their classroom. And remember, how educators respond to SEB errors can significantly impact whether or not those errors are repeated.

Implicit Bias and Disproportionate Discipline

Implicit biases are the unconscious attitudes or beliefs we hold about a group of people based on influences and experiences throughout our lives. Our implicit biases can unintentionally impact how we interact with and respond to our students. Consider these examples:

- When you need to move a bookshelf in the classroom, you ask a male student rather than a female student.
- When asking a critical thinking question, you avoid calling on the student with an IEP.

♦ During cafeteria duty, you make snap discipline decisions about the 6th-grade class because you have been told "they are a handful."

Even with the best intentions, educators can be influenced by their own implicit biases, especially when it comes to responding to SEB errors (Okonofua & Eberhardt, 2015). Furthermore, when educators' internal states are negatively impacted by conditions such as fatigue, hunger, or being overwhelmed, they are more likely to be impacted by their implicit biases (Austin et al., 2024). In addition, disciplinary decisions are more likely to be impacted by our implicit biases if a behavior is of a more subjective nature such as defiance, disrespect, and disruption (Girvan et al., 2017). This may be why we see chronic discipline disproportionality for students of color and/or students with disabilities (see Table 3.5).

TABLE 3.5 Research on Discipline Disproportionality

	What Does the Research Say?
U.S. Department of Education Office for Civil Rights, 2023	Students with disabilities represent 14% of the K-12 population; however, they were overrepresented in exclusionary discipline outcomes. • 18% of students with disabilities received one or more in-school suspensions • 24% of students with disabilities received one or more out-of-school suspensions • 17% of students with disabilities received expulsions Significant disproportionality exists across race and gender: • Black boys are almost twice as likely to receive one or more in-school suspensions and more than twice as likely to receive one or more out-of-school suspensions or be expelled than their white male peers. • Except for Black girls who were slightly over-represented, girls of other races were less under-represented in exclusionary discipline outcomes than their male peers.
Austin et al., 2024	Physical aggression, along with subjective behaviors including defiance and disruption, are the behaviors most likely to have disproportional rates of office discipline referrals for Black students compared to all other students. Disproportionate outcomes for Black students are more likely to occur during midday and afternoons.

As an educator, it is important to have awareness of these patterns and recognize ways to lessen the impact of our implicit biases. The simple act of counting to 10 or taking a few deep breaths before responding to a student's SEB error can help an educator respond more equitably to the error.

De-escalation Strategies

Everyone can experience intense emotions due to a variety of triggers, and not everyone responds to triggers the same way. By building positive, supportive relationships with our students, we can learn what triggers them and strive to prevent an escalated response. Some students are equipped either to remain relatively regulated or to use calming techniques to return them to a regulated state upon being triggered. Others are more prone to respond to triggers with agitation, yelling, physical aggression, disruption, or other escalated behaviors and may not have the skills needed to regulate themselves. Educators who understand the escalation cycle and use de-escalation strategies can provide effective support when needed (Colvin & Scott, 2014; Strickland-Cohen et al., 2022). Table 3.6 presents the seven phases of escalation, typical associated behaviors, and strategies educators can use within each phase to provide support (Strickland-Cohen et al., 2022).

You will inevitably experience episodes of escalated student behavior during your student teaching experience. Remember to be mindful of student triggers, and proactively teach students SEB skills such as calming routines and self-regulation strategies. If a student becomes agitated, use the de-escalation strategies above to support the student as needed. Rely on your cooperating teacher and other school personnel during peak phases. Look for opportunities to engage in the debriefing session after the student recovers.

Key Takeaways

♦ *Before identifying a pattern of SEB errors as a student problem, consider the strength of your key Tier 1 practices to support SEB expectations and skills.*

TABLE 3.6 Phases of the Escalation Cycle and Relevant Support Strategies

Escalation Cycle Phase	Typical Student Characteristics	Support Strategies
Calm	• Cooperative • Responsive • Using needed SEB and academic skills	• Focus on prevention by teaching, prompting, and reinforcing SEB skills, including calming techniques and self-regulation strategies • Maintain high rates of active academic engagement • Problem-solve chronic SEB errors
Trigger	• Student becomes upset, dysregulated, angry, sad, frustrated, or anxious, or experiences other unsettled emotions, due to something within the environment	• Remind student of previously taught calming techniques and self-regulation strategies • Redirect student to another engaging activity • When possible, offer choice of ways to respond to the trigger
Agitation	• SEB errors begin to occur • May begin to increase movement and/or blurt • Has difficulty attending to instruction	• Connect empathetically with the student • Offer help • Use proximity to monitor student needs • Repeat prompts encouraging calming techniques and self-regulation strategies
Acceleration	• SEB errors intensify • Off-task • Movement intensifies • Work refusal	• Offer space while student remains supervised • Reduce verbal interaction • Reinforce demonstrated use of SEB skills
Peak	• Physical aggression • Yelling • Damages property • Threatens others • Elopement	• Prioritize safety • Use crisis/safety protocols • Stay calm and neutral • Use few words and avoid demands
De-escalation	• SEB errors decrease • Confused/fatigued • Withdrawn • May blame others	• Provide recovery time preferably in a calm, quiet space • Slowly return to routine and offer a low-demand activity • Reinforce use of SEB skills

Recovery	• May attempt to repair harm
	• Return to a calm state
		• Consider ways to repair harm
		• Debrief the event
		   • Identify trigger
		   • Make a plan for next time

- *Focus on an instructional approach to SEB errors. Strive for the least intensive response that will have the greatest impact.*
- *Deliver corrections respectfully, calmly, and privately.*
- *Recognize that our own implicit biases may impact our responses to students' SEB errors, particularly during midday and afternoon, or when faced with subjective behaviors such as defiance and disruption.*
- *Whenever possible, be mindful of and work to prevent triggers known to escalate student behavior. If escalated behavior occurs, use de-escalation strategies.*

Perspectives in Practice: Stepping into the Role and Promoting a Welcoming Classroom Environment

Even though Ann started her first day of student teaching in the first-grade classroom with manageable nerves, she was faced with a jumble of confusion. She was ready to tackle her in-classroom experience but wasn't sure where to start. Unsure of whether to assist her cooperating teacher or to hang back and observe, Ann was hesitant to step in. On top of that, Ann realized, each classroom runs slightly differently, each with its own unique rules, routines, and expectations. How was she supposed to fit into it all?

Ann was in a completely new environment, surrounded by children she never met before, but she realized that this was her opportunity to learn how to actually interact with students. After all the hypothetical scenarios she had in her college courses, she noted that the application of skills learned through college coursework is challenging when actually in a real classroom. So, Ann started by connecting with her students. She listened to them, which built a sense of trust and would make it easier for them to come to her if they struggle. She reassured them with reminders like, "Nobody is born perfect" and "When I was your age, I wasn't able to do that." This helped Ann build connections with her students, which is an essential starting point in the classroom.

New student teacher, Raven, also found herself hesitating to take on a leading role in the classroom, and what she found most helpful was getting hands-on with any small task. "Printing, laminating, cutting, copying, anything in the classroom—all that experience will help you," Raven noted. Even seemingly mundane tasks incorporate you into the classroom environment and help the students gain comfort with and respect for you. So don't shy away! No matter your starting point, there are plenty of opportunities for you to establish your presence in the classroom as a welcoming person who can foster the best classroom environment.

Mentorship Corner: Setting Everyone Up for Success

Tips for Cooperating Teachers
- Review and model teaching and re-teaching your class expectations, routines, and procedures with your student teacher. Involve your student teacher in this process.
- Review and model strategies used for reinforcing appropriate behavior, such as positive, contingent feedback. Assist your student teacher with planning to incorporate reinforcement strategies in their lessons.
- When you need to respond to behavioral errors, share your thought process with your student teacher. Discuss how you responded instructionally to the SEB error and how you will support SEB skill use in the future.
- Just as cooperating teachers typically provide a gradual release of academic responsibility, provide a gradual release of SEB support responsibility. (Be explicit!) Consider this example:
    - Week 1: Student teacher greets students at the door
    - Week 2: Student teacher provides prompts before transitions
    - Week 3: Student teacher monitors students during individual work time and provides specific feedback
    - Week 4: Student teacher provides specific praise to students throughout group instruction
    - Week 5: Student teacher reteaches classroom expectations to the whole group
    - Week 6: Student teacher is responsible for a class-wide acknowledgment system

♦ Observe your student teacher's implementation of Tier 1 practices. Provide specific feedback on their use of these strategies. Work together to identify areas to strengthen and develop a plan for improvement.

Tips for University Supervisors
♦ Discuss the rationale for using positive, proactive classroom management strategies with your student teacher during pre-observation meetings. Tell your student teacher specific practices you plan to observe (teaching expectations, providing positive and contingent feedback, etc.).
♦ During your observation, collect data on the use of observable practices such as prompts, specific praise, and a positive-to-corrective interaction ratio.
♦ Provide specific feedback and help your student teacher to reflect on their own use of practices to support a positive learning environment.
♦ Communicate with cooperating teachers regularly. Share program goals for your student teacher in the area of the classroom environment. Provide support to your cooperating teachers as needed.
♦ Consider using video models and video analysis to aid this process. See the "Teacher Toolbox" for more information on observation tools and video modeling resources.

Practice and Reflect: Application Activities to Support Your Development

In Your Classroom

- Pay close attention to how your cooperating teacher teaches and reteaches classroom expectations, works to develop positive relationships with students, and provides feedback to students on their behavior. What specific strategies do you observe? How can you incorporate these strategies into your lesson plans?

- Set aside time to informally observe your cooperating teacher. During observations collect frequency data on key SEB practices. During observations, tally instances of prompting for expectations, providing various opportunities to respond, and offering contingent, specific feedback. Additionally, reflect on the cooperating teacher's use of proximity and active supervision. Note changes in student behavior based on your cooperating teacher's use of these key practices.
- Practice pausing before responding to a student's SEB error to ensure you are responding intentionally.

In Seminar or Post-observation Meetings

- Consider using "COACHED" (see Teacher Toolbox) to provide specific feedback to your student teacher on the implementation of key practices that support a positive and predictable learning environment. In post-observation meetings, share data-based feedback with your student teacher to prompt reflection on these practices. Work together to set goals for future observations.
- Discuss ways to pause and reflect before making a disciplinary decision.
- Role-play the escalation cycle and practice de-escalation strategies.

On Your Own

- Use video self-analysis to monitor your practice. What strategies do you use to create a productive, positive learning environment? How do you work to engage all students in activities? In what ways do you want to improve your practice?
- Consider when you are most likely to make snap disciplinary decisions and develop a strategy for responding more intentionally.

Teacher Toolbox: Resources for Further Exploration

1. High Leverage Practices for Inclusive Classrooms (highleveragepractices.org).[1] Watch HLP #7 "Establish a consistent, organized, and respectful learning environment" and HLP #8 "Provide positive and constructive feedback to guide students' learning and behavior."
2. *Supporting and Responding to Students' Social, Emotional, and Behavioral Needs*: Evidence-Based Practices for Educators developed[2] through the Center on PBIS.
3. *IRIS Center Module*: Classroom and Behavior Management (Part 1) Key Concepts and Foundational Practices.[3]
4. *The Teaching Channel (requires subscription)*: Caring and Control Create a Safe and Positive Classroom.[4]

5. *COACHED*[5]: Use this observational tool to collect data and provide specific feedback on key classroom management practices. This includes several Project FRaME Content Acquisition Podcast video models of specific practices. These can also be found on www.spedintro.com.[6]
6. Strategies for De-escalating Student Behavior in the Classroom[7] offers insight and strategies for educators to use throughout all phases of the escalation cycle.

Notes

1. https://highleveragepractices.org/
2. https://www.pbis.org/resource/supporting-and-responding-to-behavior-evidence-based-classroom-strategies-for-teachers
3. https://iris.peabody.vanderbilt.edu/module/beh1/
4. https://learn.teachingchannel.com/video/create-a-safe-classroom
5. https://www.coached.education.virginia.edu/
6. http://www.spedintro.com/
7. https://www.pbis.org/resource/strategies-for-de-escalating-student-behavior-in-the-classroom

References

Aldrup, K., Klusmann, U., Lüdtke, O., Göllner, R., & Trautwein, U. (2018). Student misbehavior and teacher well-being: Testing the mediating role of the teacher-student relationship. *Learning and Instruction, 58*, 126–136.

Archer, A. L., & Hughes, C. A. (2010). *Explicit instruction: Effective and efficient teaching.* Retrieved from http://ebookcentral.proquest.com

Austin, S. C., McIntosh, K., & Girvan, E. J. (2024). National patterns of vulnerable decision points in school discipline. *Journal of School Psychology, 102*, 101259.

Caldarella, P., Larsen, R. A., Williams, L., Downs, K. R., Wills, H. P., & Wehby, J. H. (2020). Effects of teachers' praise-to-reprimand ratios on elementary students' on-task behaviour. *Educational Psychology, 40*(10), 1306–1322. https://doi.org/10.1080/01443410.2020.1711872

Caldarella, P., Larsen, R. A. A., Williams, L., Wills, H. P., & Wehby, J. H. (2021). "Stop Doing That!": Effects of teacher reprimands on student disruptive behavior and engagement. *Journal of Positive Behavior Interventions*, *23*(3), 163–173. https://doi.org/10.1177/1098300720935101

Chafouleas, S. (August 2020). Four questions to ask now in preparing your child for school. *Psychology Today*. https://www.psychologytoday.com/us/blog/promoting-student-well-being/202008/4questions-ask-now-in-preparing-your-child-school

Cheryan, S., Ziegler, S. A., Plaut, V. C., & Meltzoff, A. N. (2014). Designing classrooms to maximize student achievement. *Policy Insights from the Behavioral and Brain Sciences*, *1*(1), 4–12.

Colvin, G., & Scott, T. M. (2014). *Managing the cycle of acting-out behavior in the classroom*. Corwin Press.

Colvin, G., Sugai, G., Good, R. H. III, & Lee, Y. Y. (1997). Using active supervision and precorrection to improve transition behaviors in an elementary school. *School Psychology Quarterly*, *12*(4), 344.

Condliffe, B., Zhu, P., Doolittle, F., van Dok, M., Power, H., Denison, D., & Kurki, A. (2022). *Study of training in multi-tiered systems of support for behavior: Impacts on elementary school students' outcomes.* Appendix. NCEE 2022-008a. *National Center for Education Evaluation and Regional Assistance*.

Cook, C. R., Fiat, A., Larson, M., Daikos, C., Slemrod, T., Holland, E. A., & Renshaw, T. (2018). Positive greetings at the door: Evaluation of a low-cost, high-yield proactive classroom management strategy. *Journal of Positive Behavior Interventions*, *20*(3), 149–159.

Cook, C. R., Grady, E. A., Long, A. C., Renshaw, T., Codding, R. S., Fiat, A., & Larson, M. (2017). Evaluating the impact of increasing general education teachers' ratio of positive-to-negative interactions on students' classroom behavior. *Journal of Positive Behavior Interventions*, *19*(2), 67–77. https://doi.org/10.1177/1098300716679137

Cooper, J. O., Heron, T. E., & Heward, W. L. (2020). *Applied behavior analysis* (3rd ed.). Pearson.

Ennis, R. P., Jolivette, K., & Losinski, M. (2017). The effects of writing choice prompt on the written narratives of students with emotional and behavioral disorders: A case study of an abandoned single-case design. *Behavioral Disorders*, *42*(4), 185–195.

Gage, N. A., Haydon, T., MacSuga-Gage, A. S., Flowers, E., & Erdy, L. (2020). An evidence-based review and meta-analysis of active supervision. *Behavioral Disorders*, *45*(2), 117–128.

Gage, N. A., & MacSuga-Gage, A. S. (2017). Salient classroom management skills: Finding the most effective skills to increase student engagement and decrease disruptions. *Report on Emotional & Behavioral Disorders in Youth*, *17*(1), 13–18.

Girvan, E. J., Gion, C., McIntosh, K., & Smolkowski, K. (2017). The relative contribution of subjective office referrals to racial disproportionality in school discipline. *School Psychology Quarterly*, *32*(3), 392.

Haring, N. G., Lovitt, T. C., Eaton, M. D., & Hansen, C. L. (1978). *The fourth R: Research in the classroom*. Charles E. Merrill Publishing Company.

Haydon, T., Hunter, W., & Scott, T. M. (2019). Active supervision: Preventing behavioral problems before they occur. *Beyond Behavior*, *28*(1), 29–35. https://doi.org/10.1177/1074295619835190

Herman, K. C., Hickmon-Rosa, J. E., & Reinke, W. M. (2018). Empirically derived profiles of teacher stress, burnout, self-efficacy, and coping and associated student outcomes. *Journal of Positive Behavior Interventions*, *20*(2), 90–100.

Longobardi, C., Prino, L. E., Marengo, D., & Settanni, M. (2016). Student-teacher relationships as a protective factor for school adjustment during the transition from middle to high school. *Frontiers in Psychology*, *7*, 1988.

Martin, A. J., & Collie, R. J. (2019). Teacher–student relationships and students' engagement in high school: Does the number of negative and positive relationships with teachers matter? *Journal of Educational Psychology*, *111*(5), 861–876. https://doi.org/10.1037/edu0000317

O'Connor, E. E., Dearing, E., & Collins, B. A. (2011). Teacher-child relationship and behavior problem trajectories in elementary school. *American Educational Research Journal*, *48*(1), 120–162. https://doi-org.ezproxy.lib.uconn.edu/10.3102/0002831210365008

Okonofua, J. A., & Eberhardt, J. L. (2015). Two strikes: Race and the disciplining of young students. *Psychological Science*, *26*(5), 617–624. https://doi.org/10.1177/0956797615570365

Reinke, W. M., Herman, K. C., & Stormont, M. (2013). Classroom-level positive behavior supports in schools implementing SW-PBIS:

Identifying areas for enhancement. *Journal of Positive Behavior Interventions*, *15*(1), 39–50.

Reinke, W. M., Lewis-palmer, T., & Merrell, K. (2008). The classroom check-up: A classwide teacher. *School Psychology Review*, *37*(3), 315–332. https://doi.org/10.1016/j.biotechadv.2011.08.021.

Rodrigues, P. F., & Pandeirada, J. N. (2018). When visual stimulation of the surrounding environment affects children's cognitive performance. *Journal of Experimental Child Psychology*, *176*, 140–149.

Sabey, C. V., Charlton, C., & Charlton, S. R. (2019). The "magic" positive-to-negative interaction ratio: Benefits, applications, cautions, and recommendations. *Journal of Emotional and Behavioral Disorders*, *27*(3), 154–164. https://doi.org/10.1177/1063426618763106

Scott, T. M. (2016). *Teaching behavior: Managing classrooms through effective instruction*. Corwin Press.

Simonsen, B., Fairbanks, S., Briesch, A., Myers, D., & Sugai, G. (2008). Evidence-based practices in classroom management: Considerations for research to practice. *Education & Treatment of Children*, *31*(3), 351–380.

Simonsen, B., Freeman, J., Dooley, K., Maddock, E., Kern, L., & Myers, D. (2017). Effects of targeted professional development on teachers' specific praise rates. *Journal of Positive Behavior Interventions*, *19*(1), 37–47.

Strickland-Cohen, mK., Newson, A., Meyer, K., Putnam, R., Kern, L., Meyer, B. C., & Flammini, A. (September, 2022). *Strategies for de-escalating student behavior in the classroom*. Center on PBIS, University of Oregon. www.pbis.org

U.S. Department of Education Office for Civil Rights. (2023). *2020-21 Civil Rights Data Collection: Student Discipline and School Climate in U.S. Public Schools*. https://www2.ed.gov/about/offices/list/ocr/docs/crdc-discipline-school-climate-report.pdf

Wills, H. P., Caldarella, P., Williams, L., Fleming, K., & Chen, P.-Y. (2023). Middle school classroom management: A randomized control trial of class-wide function-related intervention teams for middle schools (CW-FIT MS). *Journal of Behavioral Education*, *32*(2), 189–211. https://doi.org/10.1007/s10864-021-09455-0

4

Positive Student Behavior Support Practices

Tyler is a seventh grader who excels in most of their classes. However, Tyler finds their foreign language class challenging and frequently engages in disruptive behavior, such as talking to peers, drumming on the desk, and refusing to complete assignments. Tyler's student teacher, Ms. Sutton, provides brief, specific corrections, redirects, and conferences with Tyler as needed. While these instructional approaches have helped, the disruptive behavior has continued. Some days the disruptions are so significant that Ms. Sutton sends Tyler down to the office. Ms. Sutton, with guidance from her cooperating teacher, reached out to the school's Advanced Tiers behavior support team to get further insight into how to meet Tyler's SEB needs in her class.

Even with the best intentions, and even with educators who use evidence-based Tier 1 social, emotional, or behavioral (SEB) support practices at high rates, some students will need additional support to be successful in the classroom. This chapter will offer guidance on how to know whether you are implementing key practices with fidelity, provide a basic explanation of behavioral science, demonstrate how to effectively use data for decision-making, and support you in providing targeted and individualized behavior support.

Why Do We Need to Know How to Support Students with Advanced SEB Support Needs?

Let's start by recognizing that all students in our classrooms are our students! As an educator, you may need additional support to meet the needs of a diverse group of learners; however, if they are on your roster, you have a role to play in their success, even for students with significant behavior support needs, IEPs, or 504 plans. Remember, the goal is to maximize instructional time within the classroom and keep students in the least restrictive environment as much as possible. Therefore, effective support of Tier 2 and 3 SEB needs relies on the general education teacher's competency in a wide range of positive behavior support practices. Because not all students needing additional SEB support are identified at the start of the year and circumstances continuously change, general educators must also be adept at differentiating and intensifying key Tier 1 strategies and capturing student data to determine when and if additional supports may be needed. It sounds like a lot, and it is. However, it can be done if you already know the key practices, understand the basics of behavior science, use simple data collection tools, and collaborate with other professionals when needed!

Background Considerations for Advanced SEB Support

Educator Fidelity Matters

Ms. Sutton knows it is important to identify and explicitly teach the SEB skills expected in the classroom. She and her cooperating teacher use role-plays to model and practice routines such as passing in work, having group discussions, and gathering instructional materials within the room. She also works hard on developing lessons where students have various ways to engage with the instruction. She greets students at the door, fosters positive relationships, and tries to provide more positive than corrective feedback. When students make academic or SEB errors, she delivers brief corrections, redirects them, and conferences with students as needed. Her cooperating teacher has told her she has strong classroom management skills. Most of the students in her classes are doing well, so why is Tyler struggling?

Ms. Sutton was right to self-assess her own instructional practices before assuming Tyler was "just a tough student to manage." Classrooms are busy places! Educators may have the best intentions of implementing the key practices discussed in Chapter 3 but may struggle with providing them consistently or at a high enough rate to make a positive impact. For example, numerous research studies demonstrate that, even with explicit professional development on maintaining a 5:1 positive-to-negative interaction rate with students, most educators struggle to consistently reach and maintain that ratio (Cook et al., 2017; Hagermoser Sanetti et al., 2018; Reinke et al., 2013). Table 4.1 offers further insight into each of these studies.

If educators notice more than 20% of their students consistently engaging in contextually inappropriate behavior, they should step back and evaluate their use of key practices. It can be really helpful to have a peer observe a lesson and collect data, such as rates of opportunities to respond, rates of specific praise, or rates of positive-to-negative interactions (see Table 4.2). Receiving specific feedback is as helpful to educators as it is for students learning new content! If a peer is unavailable, educators

TABLE 4.1 Research on Strategies to Strengthen Teacher Practices

	What Does the Research Say?
Cook et al., 2017	Teachers who received explicit training in providing a high rate of positive-to-corrective interactions improved their ratio; however, they struggled to maintain the improvement over time. Teachers in the control group consistently had a low ratio of positive-to-corrective interactions.
Hagermoser Sanetti et al., 2018	Teachers receiving consultation about evidence-based classroom management practices improved their adherence to an implementation plan but, at 1- and 2-month follow-ups, adherence to and quality of the plan decreased.
Reinke et al., 2013	In schools reaching fidelity with schoolwide PBIS, many teachers continued to struggle with maintaining a high ratio of positive-to-negative interactions with students.

TABLE 4.2 Sample Tally Chart of Key Practices

Minutes Observed	15		
Prompts	III	Opportunities to Respond	ℍℍ II
Specific Praise	III	Specific Correction	ℍℍ II
General Praise	ℍℍ IIII	General Correction	ℍℍ ℍℍ III

can self-monitor by using a counter, marking tallies, or recording themselves during instruction.

If less than 20% of students are experiencing challenges, the educator is likely implementing key Tier 1 behavior support practices with fidelity, and some students simply need targeted or individualized support. The key is considering educator fidelity before assuming the problem lies in the student or students.

Behavior Is Contextual

People are not born knowing how to behave appropriately in any given circumstance, and behavior does not happen in a vacuum. Behavior is a form of communication learned through repeated practice as we recognize what does and does not work to support our goals. Our understanding of appropriate behavior within a given context develops due to a learning history based on our experiences, culture, and relationships. As a result, behaviors should not be considered bad or good but rather contextually inappropriate or appropriate. Let's consider some examples. When a family member reads to a young child at home, the child is typically encouraged to ask questions, point out connections, and actively engage with the pictures in the book. If that same young child demonstrates those same behaviors during a classroom read-aloud, it is likely called blurting and disrupting. Yelling is not appropriate in the cafeteria, but it is appropriate 5 minutes later at recess. Helping peers with their work during a group project is acceptable; during an exam, it is not. All behavior can be appropriate in the right context. Moving away from subjective terms such as good or bad helps educators to be culturally responsive, inclusive of their students' learning histories and promotes greater use of explicit teaching of contextually appropriate behavior.

Basic Behavioral Theory

To effectively support students' behavioral needs, it is helpful to understand some foundational components of behavioral science (Baer et al., 1968; Cooper et al., 2020; Skinner, 1953). In this section, we will explain the three-term contingency model, examine how reinforcement and punishment impact future behavior, explore the function of behavior, and address some common misconceptions. Please know that we provide only a brief, simplified overview of these concepts. Each of these areas could take up entire chapters! At the end of this chapter, there are multiple resources to support your further exploration. Let's get started.

Three-term Contingency Model

As mentioned earlier, behavior does not occur in a vacuum. It is learned, and it is a form of communication. When identifying behavior, it is important to identify what can be observed and measured rather than relying on emotions or assumptions. For example, a student who puts their head on their desk during independent work might be feeling tired, frustrated, overwhelmed, or any other emotion. Rather than making assumptions, notice what the student is actually doing as you apply the three-term contingency model. The science of behavior (Skinner, 1953) claims that for every behavior, something happens right before the behavior to trigger the behavior to occur. This is called an antecedent. Additionally, something occurs immediately after as a result of the behavior. This is called the consequence. These three components work together to form the three-term contingency model (e.g., Cooper et al., 2020). Table 4.3 provides some examples.

What happens as a consequence of a behavior determines whether or not that behavior is likely to occur again in the future. This leads us to the concepts of reinforcement and punishment.

Consequences: Reinforcing or Punishing?

Now that we have a basic understanding of how the three-term contingency model works, let's explore the impact of consequences.

TABLE 4.3 Examples of the Three-Term Contingency Model

Antecedent	Behavior	Consequence
Educator rings a bell	Students stop talking	Classroom is quiet
Coach tells players to begin laps	Players run	Players are warmed up for practice
Driver sees a red traffic light	Driver presses the brake pedal	Driver stops at intersection
Educator hands student an assignment	Student pushes paper away	Educator asks "What is wrong?"
Parent says "No" when child asks for a cookie	Child falls to floor, kicks and screams	Parent leaves the room

A common misunderstanding is that "consequences" always indicate something bad or aversive and that a "consequence" is synonymous with punishment. However, a consequence can be either reinforcing or punishing. When a behavior results in a pleasant or desirable experience (consequence), it will likely occur again. In other words, the behavior has been reinforced. In contrast, if a behavior results in an unpleasant or aversive experience (consequence), the behavior is less likely to occur again. This means the behavior has been punished.

Educators will want to reinforce contextually appropriate classroom behaviors and punish contextually inappropriate classroom behaviors. Please note, however, that punishing does not have to lead to removal from instruction, more work, loss of privilege, etc. Rather, punishing may mean ignoring behavior or removing something desirable. Punishing should only occur within an environment containing a high level of reinforcement. Chapter 3 offers multiple strategies for reinforcement and instructional responses to SEB errors.

Function of Behavior

You may be asking, how do I know what is reinforcing or punishing to a student? Isn't that dependent on student preferences? The answer is YES! We can generalize that most students value specific praise and educator attention; however, that may not be true for all students. For example, a middle school student may or may not appreciate being recognized publicly at a school assembly for their accomplishments. Recognizing what is reinforcing vs. punishing for your students requires you to get to know your students through positive connections, observations over time, and an understanding of the function of behavior.

Remember, behavior is a form of communication and behavior occurs to either obtain or avoid something. A person may engage in a particular behavior because they may be trying to get a tangible item, activity, attention, or sensory experience. Or, they may be trying to escape from any of those same things. When a behavior works to help someone accomplish the goal of obtaining or avoiding something, the behavior has been reinforced. The opposite is true if the behavior does not help someone achieve their goal. In that case, the behavior is punished and less likely to occur again. Skilled educators use these principles to strengthen contextually appropriate classroom behaviors and diminish contextually inappropriate classroom behaviors. Let's go back to Tyler and Mrs. Sutton for an example of how to apply the three-term contingency model, analyze consequences, and hypothesize a possible function of behavior in the classroom.

Tyler finds foreign language learning really hard. When they complete assignments, there are many errors and blanks. In addition, they have failed quizzes and are in danger of failing the class altogether. The Advanced Behavior Support team asked Ms. Sutton to gather some A-B-C data about what happens immediately before (A-antecedent) and immediately after (C-consequence) Tyler's disruptive behavior (identified as work refusal, making noises, distracting peers, etc.) (B-behavior). For one week, they captured data in an ABC chart (see Table 4.4).

What do you notice with this data? Did capturing a week's worth of A-B-C data provide any insight into Tyler's behavior? Hopefully, you are noticing a pattern. Each time Tyler is expected to complete an assignment, they engage in disruptive behavior. The disruptive behavior continues daily, so the behavior is being reinforced. To understand how it is being reinforced, we must consider the function of Tyler's behavior. What are they trying to obtain or avoid? Based on the consequences of their behavior, we can hypothesize that they are seeking to avoid completing

TABLE 4.4 Sample A-B-C Data for Tyler

Antecedent	Behavior	Consequence
An assignment is handed to Tyler	Pushes paper away, places head down on desk	Assignment not completed
Ms. Sutton begins explaining the independent practice assignment to be completed in class	Talks loudly and disruptively with nearby students	Does not hear directions for the assignment, so is unable to complete it without support from Ms. Sutton
Students are asked to write an entry in their journal	Tells Ms. Sutton they will not do any more writing today	Sent to the office
Students are given time to catch up on work and receive help	Loudly drums the desk with fingers (enough to disrupt nearby peers)	Conferences with Ms. Sutton and does not complete the assignment
An assignment is handed to Tyler	Pushes the paper away, gets up from the desk, and walks out of the room	Sent to the office

difficult assignments, and it worked! Knowing this information, Ms. Sutton can work on providing a different response to their disruptive behavior such as providing space for Tyler to get increased support, reteaching relevant skills, and offering frequent reinforcement when Tyler is actively engaged. The key is to be sure Tyler's behavior does not result in an escape from completing assignments.

Performance or Skill Deficit?

As we just explained, when someone is engaging in contextually inappropriate behavior, educators need to consider the function of the behavior. Additionally, educators must consider whether or not the student's behavior results from a performance or skill deficit.

Performance deficits occur when a person has all the skills they need to engage in contextually appropriate behavior, but they do not do it. There are numerous reasons why someone might not engage in a behavior. Looking at the behavior across time and considering its function offers educators a way to intervene effectively (Gage et al., 2012).

Skill deficits, however, result from not having the skills needed to engage in a contextually appropriate behavior. For example, since Tyler is successful in all other classes, they are likely engaging in disruptive behavior to avoid tasks requiring skills they don't currently have. Tyler may have some academic skill deficits in this particular content area. Perhaps Tyler would benefit from targeted small group work in foreign languages to bolster their skills and capacity. Perhaps Tyler has not experienced academic challenges before and does not know how to persevere through hard things, ask for help, or accept mistakes as a part of learning. If so, Tyler is experiencing some SEB skill deficits. Just as academic skill deficits can be overcome with targeted reteaching, so can SEB skill deficits. Tyler may benefit from any combination of social-emotional learning supports, including frequent check-ins, higher reinforcement rates, and explicit instruction in formulating contextually appropriate responses to hard demands.

Both performance and skill deficits may require some targeted, or Tier 2, support; and, if Tier 2 support doesn't address the deficits or positively impact the contextually inappropriate behavior patterns, then Tier 3 support, or intensive and individualized support, may be necessary. The next section addresses these advanced support tiers.

Key Takeaways

- *Educator fidelity to effective Tier 1 practices should be the first consideration when trying to understand student behavior challenges.*
- *Behavior is a form of communication. It is learned over time, adapts to varied contexts, and can be changed through consistent instructional strategies.*
- *To understand why a person is behaving a certain way, it is important to notice what happens immediately before (antecedent) and after (consequence) a behavior over time so you can determine the function, or purpose, of the behavior. Behavior occurs to either obtain or avoid something.*

Supporting Students Who Need Advanced Behavior Support

Tier 2 Support

The A-B-C data collected helped Ms. Sutton, her cooperating teacher, and the advanced behavior support team gather insight into Tyler's ongoing disruptive behavior. As a first Tier 2 support step, the team has decided to provide targeted, small group instruction in foreign language to bolster Tyler's skills, paired with increased frequency of specific praise during class. Ms. Sutton was asked to continue to capture data on the frequency of Tyler's behavior to determine if the intervention decreases the disruptive behavior (see Table 4.4).

Tier 2 should be an intensification and more targeted delivery of Tier 1 practices, such as providing explicit instruction, specific feedback, prompting, opportunities to respond and practice, and supportive check-ins. Tier 2 support does not need to be something different from what is provided in Tier 1, and it is often provided within the classroom setting. Some schools offer more formalized schoolwide Tier 2 support such as Check-In/Check Out (Hawken et al., 2020), Breaks are Better (Anderson & Boyd, 2011), or social skills instruction groups. You can learn more about schoolwide Tier 2 interventions in this chapter's Teacher Toolbox.

To provide Tier 2 support, Ms. Sutton adds Tyler to her small group instruction classroom routine during independent work time. Additionally, she intentionally provides high rates of specific praise to Tyler and monitors her fidelity by keeping a tally sheet on a clipboard she carries around the room (see Table 4.5). Over time, Tyler begins to increase his fluency in the skills needed to be successful with assignments, and the disruptive behavior decreases.

Ms. Sutton continued to provide small group instruction and high rates of specific praise to Tyler for 6 weeks. Over time, Tyler's disruptive behavior continued to decrease until it happened less than once each week. At the same time, Tyler's foreign language skills improved, and they began successfully completing assignments independently. Ms. Sutton reduced Tyler's small group time to 1–2 times per week and continued to provide high rates of specific praise. Eventually, Tyler no longer needed small group support; instead, they learned how to ask for help when needed.

TABLE 4.5 Tally Sheet of Tyler's Behavior and Ms. Sutton's Specific Praise

Student Name:	Tyler	Behavior:	Disruption (Talking to Peers, Drumming on Table, Work Refusal)
Date	Number of Behavior Incidents	Specific Praise Provided	Notes
2/3	III	ℍℍ II	Small group began
2/4	II	ℍℍ ℍℍ	Small group interrupted often by peers
2/5		ℍℍ ℍℍ II	
2/8	I	ℍℍ III	
2/9	II	ℍℍ	No small group today
2/10	I	ℍℍ ℍℍ	
2/11		ℍℍ II	
2/12		ℍℍ III	
* This is a sample of the data gathered over 6 weeks.			

Tyler's experience demonstrates how data-based decision-making, attention to the function of behavior, and targeted, intensified Tier 1 practices can be used to implement a successful Tier 2 intervention. Some students may require ongoing Tier 2 support, whereas others may need Tier 2 support for a short time. Remember to continue to capture simple data to guide your decision-making! A common mistake occurs when educators stop providing Tier 2 support too abruptly or too soon. Rather, gradually reduce support if the student continues to meet the desired goals. If Tier 2 supports are implemented with fidelity and the student continues to experience challenges, it is likely time to consider a Tier 3 level of support.

Tier 3 Support

Tier 3 support, or intensive, individualized support, is for students who are not responding to Tier 1 and 2 practices. It is also for students engaging in dangerous or highly disruptive behaviors that impact the safety and efficacy of the learning environment. A student needing Tier 3 support does not automatically require special education services. Ideally, your school will have a team and/or service providers such as counselors, behavior interventionists, social workers, and special education staff available to consult with general education teachers about students requiring Tier 3 support; however, if your school does not, do not worry! In this next section, we will provide a brief overview of how you can strengthen your own use of Tier 3 support practices to meet your student needs. There are many resources in the Teacher Toolkit section of this chapter if you want to go deeper.

Like Tier 2, Tier 3 support requires data-based decision-making and an understanding of the function of the behavior. Additionally, Tier 3 support may include layering additional supports to address specific needs. Whenever possible, the student and their family should be involved in developing an individualized behavior support plan (BSP), which will enhance the student's quality of life and promote positive outcomes.

An effective BSP begins with a hypothesis identifying an observable, measurable description of the concerning behavior, when the behavior is likely to occur, why a behavior is occurring, and how it is being reinforced. Typically, a trained behavior analyst will complete a functional behavioral assessment (FBA) (Crone et al., 2015). If that is not available, you can use A-B-C data you collect over time. Consider the following example hypotheses:

- When the bell rings to signal the end of recess, Maddie runs into the woods to avoid coming inside.
- When handed an assignment, Jamie puts their head down on the desk and pushes the paper onto the floor to avoid completing the work.
- When the teacher is providing whole group instruction, Matt blurts and calls out repeatedly to gain attention from the teacher.

Educators use that hypothesis to develop a BSP that prevents the concerning behavior from happening, teaches alternative behaviors, reinforces contextually appropriate behavior, and instructionally responds to SEB errors. Table 4.6 provides a sample BSP incorporating critical elements to support the

TABLE 4.6 Sample Behavior Support Plan

Student:	Maddie Parsons	Teacher:	Mr. Garrison
Behavior Support Plan			
Hypothesis	When the bell rings to signal the end of recess, Maddie runs into the woods to avoid coming inside.		
Prevention strategies	A recess monitor will: • provide Maddie with a 5-minute warning before recess ends • prompt Maddie to get into line when the bell rings		
Alternative behaviors to be taught	How to get into line at the end of recess		
Reinforcement of contextually appropriate behavior	Maddie will receive specific praise and add a checkmark to her reinforcement chart every time she gets into line at the end of recess rather than run into the woods. When Maddie receives 3 checkmarks, she will earn an extra 10 minutes of recess.		
Instructional response to SEB error	If Maddie runs into the woods at the end of recess, a recess monitor will bring her back to the playground, lead her to where her class lines up, and ask her to demonstrate walking into the school. • Safety is the first priority! If Maddie refuses to leave the woods, call for the support team. • If Maddie is safe but refuses to practice lining up and walking into the school, the behavior interventionist will relieve the recess monitor and engage in a problem-solving conversation with Maddie.		
Progress Monitoring			

Week Of	3/3	3/10	3/17	3/24	3/31	4/7
# of Incidents	5	3	1	2	1	0

Implementation Fidelity

	When?	By Who?	Completed?
Teaching of alternative behaviors	Initial: 3/2 during recess Follow up: 3/5 during recess	Behavior Interventionist	Yes Yes

Mark the Degree of Implementation and the Date Daily

N = Not at all P = Partially F = Fully * = Extra recess earned	Mon.	Tues.	Wed.	Thurs.	Fri.	
	3/3 P	3/4 P	3/5 F*	3/6 F	3/7 N	Substitute on Friday
	3/10 F	3/11 P*	3/12 F	3/13 P	3/14 P	Forgetting to complete reinforcement chart
	3/17 F*	3/18 F	3/19 F	3/20 N*	3/21 P	Assembly on Thursday no recess
	3/24 P	3/25 F*	3/26 F	3/27 F	3/28 F*	Things are going well!
	3/31 F	4/1 F	4/2 F*	4/3 P	4/4 F	Forgot to fill in chart on Thursday
	4/7 P	4/8 F*	4/9 F	4/10 F	4/11 F*	Substitute on Monday

TABLE 4.7 Research Showing the Impact of FBAs

	What Does the Research Say?
What Works Clearinghouse, 2016	This report from WWC summarizes evidence supporting the use of functional behavioral assessment-based interventions for addressing problem behavior. Across included studies, these interventions were found to have potentially positive effects on engagement and behavior.
Walker et al., 2018	Interventions implemented as a result of an FBA led to reductions in contextually inappropriate behavior and higher rates of prosocial behavior for students with disabilities in inclusive classroom environments.

student, prompts for progress monitoring, and a fidelity of implementation checklist for the educator. Keep in mind that behavior challenges are complex. This is a simplified version of a comprehensive process.

Once again, implementation fidelity is critical to student success. We cannot determine the effectiveness of an intervention if an intervention is not actually implemented. We also cannot expect students to improve their SEB skills if they are not provided the supports they need.

Individualized BSPs are one component of Tier 3 support. Table 4.7 shares some of the evidence for use of BSPs based on FBAs. Additional strategies and layers such as mental health, social work, medical, and academic support may be required. General education teachers are encouraged to partner with school counselors, nurses, social workers, interventionists, and behavior analysts to address Tier 3 student needs. As a student teacher in a general education setting, you will not be expected to conduct FBAs and develop BSPs. However, you could be asked to be a part of this process, and it is helpful to understand how plans are developed so that you feel prepared to use BSPs effectively.

Key Takeaways

- *Students who do not successfully respond to Tier 1 practices may need advanced behavior support.*

- *Tier 2 targeted support is an intensification of Tier 1 practices and can be provided by the classroom teacher. Data is needed to determine if a Tier 2 intervention is having its intended impact. Students may need Tier 2 support for a short or prolonged time before making decisions to either fade the support or move to Tier 3 support.*
- *Implementation fidelity of advanced behavior support plans is critical to positive student outcomes.*
- *Tier 3 support, or intensive and individualized support, requires observing behavior over time to determine its function. That information is used to develop a behavior support plan comprising prevention, teaching, and reinforcement strategies. Student outcomes are monitored to determine if the plan is working effectively.*

Perspectives in Practice: Advice on Establishing Yourself in the Classroom from a Cooperating Teacher's Perspective

At this point, you may have realized the unique opportunity student teaching provides by allowing you to escape the college classroom and actually engage with children in their usual environment. Leaving your familiar environment and entering the students' classroom is a major adjustment, but don't fret; your cooperating teacher knows this!

Cooperating teachers understand that supporting student behavior is a new experience for you, and they recognize that the first time in a classroom can be challenging. Haley, a cooperating teacher in a third-grade classroom, says, "I would never want a student teacher to think that they're supposed to know how to manage the classroom at the same level as their cooperating teacher. That's not a fair expectation."

Haley understands that responding to student behavior "in a real, authentic setting" is a huge component of student teaching. Especially with no prior experience with children or in a classroom, it's easy to feel lost when it comes to establishing your position in the classroom environment. This is where you can use your cooperating teacher as support! As you gradually ease into the classroom, take time to observe your cooperating teacher. And remember, you're not expected to know what to do right away.

To work through this, cooperating teachers might suggest:

- Don't take it personally: Some kids may misbehave, push your buttons, or test you, but their behavior is a function of something else. Often, they are just acting out to test the boundaries or to try to connect with you.
- Don't isolate yourself: There are likely other teachers around you going through something similar. Someone is out there who can help you, so don't fear reaching out!
- Ask lots of questions to learn about how the school supports students with advanced behavior support needs. Talk with school support personnel like counselors, interventionists, and social workers to learn more about how they collaborate with classroom teachers.
- Connect with the students who challenge you most! They are trying to communicate something and need to know an adult cares about them too.

There are constant opportunities to learn, so take it all in and don't be discouraged! It's okay to treat student teaching, and your teaching career in general, like a marathon, not a sprint. Take your time and try out different things; if something doesn't work, don't panic. Use the resources you have, and you will be okay.

Mentorship Corner: Supporting Competency with Positive Behavior Support Practices

Tips for Cooperating Teachers

- Help your student teacher monitor their fidelity to key practices (i.e., rates of specific praise, corrections, opportunities to respond) by collecting data for them.
- Share relevant student backgrounds/needs and how they relate to current student behavior.
- Support your student teacher with collecting student behavior data and implementing a behavior support plan with fidelity.

Tips for University Supervisors
- ♦ During observation, ask your student teacher about how they are supporting students with advanced behavior support needs.
- ♦ Validate/normalize challenging behavior as a source of stress, and remind student teachers about the benefits of positive behavior support on educator well-being.

Practice and Reflect: Application Activities to Support Your Development

In Your Classroom

• Choose one student who frequently engages in contextually inappropriate behavior in your classroom
    • Gather ABC data to identify the function of the behavior
    • Collaborate with your mentor teacher, other related school personnel, the student, and their family to develop an individualized behavior support plan

In Seminar or Post-observation Meetings
• Present ABC student data, discuss the possible functions of behaviors, and brainstorm potential interventions. • Share student data after BSP has been implemented. Discuss if it worked and how implementation fidelity may have impacted the outcome.
On Your Own
• Ask to join a student support meeting to learn about how the school provides advanced behavior support. • Talk with social workers and counselors in the school about their role in supporting students' SEB needs.

Teacher Toolbox: Resources for Further Exploration

- ♦ The MTSS in the Classroom guide[1] provides educators with guidance on implementing positive behavior supports across the three-tiered continuum.

- The IRIS Center[2] offers:
  - 2-part modules on *Addressing Challenging Behavior* for both elementary and secondary educators
  - Module on *Functional Behavioral Assessment: Identifying the Reasons for Problem Behavior and Developing a Behavior Plan*
- The Tier 2[3] and Tier 3[4] pages at pbis.org[5] provide an overview of each tier, why it is needed, implementation guidance, and supportive resources.
- The Strategies for De-escalating Student Behavior in the Classroom[6] practice brief presents strategies for preventing and responding to escalated behavior in the classroom.
- The Tier 3 Brief Functional Behavior Assessment (FBA) Guide[7] provides instruction on how to gather and use behavior data to develop a function-based support plan. Many resources are embedded within this guide, including data tools and BSP templates.
- Chapter 5[8] of the Missouri PBIS Tier 2 Workbook explains the purpose and procedures of Check In/Check Out as a schoolwide Tier 2 intervention.
- This Breaks Are Better Snapshot[9] outlines the components of this Tier 2 intervention.

Notes

1. https://www.pbis.org/resource/multi-tiered-system-of-supports-mtss-in-the-classroom
2. https://iris.peabody.vanderbilt.edu/pd-hours/earn-pd-hours/available-modules/
3. https://www.pbis.org/pbis/tier-2
4. https://www.pbis.org/pbis/tier-3
5. https://www.pbis.org/
6. https://www.pbis.org/resource/strategies-for-de-escalating-student-behavior-in-the-classroom

7. https://www.pbis.org/resource/tier-3-brief-functional-behavior-assessment-fba-guide
8. https://pbismissouri.org/wp-content/uploads/2017/06/5.0-MO-SW-PBS-Tier-2-Workbook-Ch-5-CICO.pdf
9. https://vkc.vumc.org/assets/files/resources/tbsp-breaks-are-better.pdf

References

Anderson, C., & Boyd, J. (2011). *Breaks are better: Implementation manual*. University of Oregon, College of Education.

Baer, D. M., Wolf, M. M., & Risley, T. R. (1968). Some current dimensions of applied behavior analysis. *Journal of Applied Behavior Analysis, 1*(1), 91.

Cook, C. R., Grady, E. A., Long, A. C., Renshaw, T., Codding, R. S., Fiat, A., & Larson, M. (2017). Evaluating the impact of increasing general education teachers' ratio of positive-to-negative interactions on students' classroom behavior. *Journal of Positive Behavior Interventions, 19*(2), 67–77. https://doi.org/10.1177/1098300716679137

Cooper, J. O., Heron, T. E., & Heward, W. L. (2020). *Applied behavior analysis*. Pearson.

Crone, D. A., Hawken, L. S., & Horner, R. H. (2015). *Building positive behavior support systems in schools: Functional behavioral assessment*. Guilford Publications.

Gage, N. A., Lewis, T. J., & Stichter, J. P. (2012). Functional behavioral assessment-based interventions for students with or at risk for emotional and/or behavioral disorders in school: A hierarchical linear modeling meta-analysis. *Behavioral Disorders, 37*(2), 55–77.

Hagermoser Sanetti, L. M., Williamson, K. M., Long, A. C. J., & Kratochwill, T. R. (2018). Increasing in-service teacher implementation of classroom management practices through consultation, implementation planning, and participant modeling. *Journal of Positive Behavior Interventions, 20*(1), 43–59. https://doi.org/10.1177/1098300717722357

Hawken, L. S., Crone, D. A., Bundock, K., & Horner, R. H. (2020). *Responding to problem behavior in schools*. Guilford Publications.

Reinke, W. M., Herman, K. C., & Stormont, M. (2013). Classroom level positive behavior supports in schools implementing SW-PBIS:

Identifying areas for enhancement. *Journal of Positive Behavior Interventions*, *15*, 39–50.

Skinner, B. F. (1953). *Science and human behavior*. Simon & Schuster.

Walker, V. L., Chung, Y.-C., & Bonnet, L. K. (2018). function-based intervention in inclusive school settings: A meta-analysis. *Journal of Positive Behavior Interventions*, *20*(4), 203–216. https://doi.org/10.1177/1098300717718350

What Works Clearinghouse (2016). Functional behavioral assessment-based interventions. *What works clearinghouse intervention report, Institute of Education Sciences*. https://ies.ed.gov/ncee/wwc/EvidenceSnapshot/667

5

Planning for Effective Instruction in the Inclusive Classroom

Ever since Monica began her fifth-grade placement, she has been looking forward to teaching science, her favorite subject area. The class is about to start a unit on the solar system, and she has studied the content, read the curriculum manual, and developed a plan for the next three weeks. Monica has already delivered her first lesson, which went okay but could have been better. She noticed that only half of the students were actively engaged throughout the lesson, and she is concerned that many of her students with diverse needs (e.g., IEPs, 504 plans, multilingual learner programming) did not achieve the lesson goals. Monica wants all her students to be successful and recognizes her crucial role in their success, so she asked her mentor teacher and university supervisor for help. They reminded her that, even though there is a manual to follow, adequate lesson preparation that includes high levels of engagement, necessary accommodations and modifications, and responsive practice activities based on diverse student abilities is still needed.

Monica's experience, which we will delve into in this chapter, is common. It highlights the complexity of effectively planning lessons for inclusive classrooms and emphasizes the need for extensive forethought, thorough preparation, and a deep understanding of diverse student abilities and needs. While it takes a lot to plan effective lessons, this challenge can be overcome with the right strategies and support. In this chapter, we will discuss the elements of an effective lesson plan, including backward design (Wiggins & McTighe, 2005), explicit instruction (Archer & Hughes, 2011), and universal design for learning (UDL) (Hall et al., 2012) principles. We will consider how to plan and prepare lessons that support high student engagement and success rates regardless of diverse student needs.

Planning for Effective Instruction

Making the most of your instructional time with students requires you to be well-prepared, and the key to preparedness is planning. You will likely notice that your cooperating teacher does not create lesson plans with the same level of detail required by your university supervisor, and you may wonder if all of your time spent planning and preparing for lessons is really necessary. Consider this story and your own similar experiences:

> *James, my 16-year-old son, passed his driver's permit test, and we've been practicing driving to prepare for his upcoming license test. Each time he gets behind the wheel, we go through a planning and preparation process. We think about the end goal and discuss various routes we might take to get there. We think through some of the challenges he might face along the way and discuss appropriate responses. We make sure the car is adjusted appropriately to meet his needs, and I provide a few reminders about safety and the rules of the road. I provide some feedback along the way while working to remain calm and, when we get home, we talk about what went well and how he might improve. Still, I remind myself, I've been a licensed driver for several decades now and my pre-driving process looks a little different. The planning and preparation required for me to drive (an expert) isn't the same as what is required for James (a novice).*

Teaching is complex and requires us to integrate content and pedagogical knowledge as we simultaneously make adjustments and respond to the unique needs of our students. For a novice teacher, this complex interaction, coupled with a lack of experience, creates a high mental load. Good planning and preparation can go a long way in helping you to manage cognitive demands during instructional delivery, which we will discuss in detail in Chapter 6. This helps you to better respond to student needs as they arise and to feel more confident in your developing practice. So, keep working on your lesson planning, with support from your cooperating teacher and university supervisor, and we promise that you will experience the benefits!

Step one of effective planning begins with knowing what you hope your students will learn. Basically, start at the end and go backward from there. As you design units and lessons, it is critical to have both short-term and long-term goals in mind. Once you know what you are hoping to achieve, you can consider the learning steps required to reach that goal so you can provide explicit instruction, including modeling and scaffolded practice opportunities, as students develop relevant skills and gain necessary knowledge. Pairing explicit instruction with the UDL framework ensures that you are supporting each and every student. This chapter, like others throughout the book, provides a brief overview of backward design, explicit instruction, and UDL. It is not intended to offer preservice educators the full breadth of training in each of these concepts. Resources are provided to learn more about each concept in the Toolbox section at the end of the chapter. Let's get started!

Backward Design

Instructional time is a valuable resource. You want to ensure you use your instructional time to meet the national, state, or local curriculum standards relevant to your school. Therefore, before developing any lesson plans, coordinate with your mentor teacher! Once you know the standards, consider how students will demonstrate meeting that standard (assessment). Then, design a series of learning experiences to guide them toward that goal. Figure 5.1 demonstrates these phases of backwards design logic.

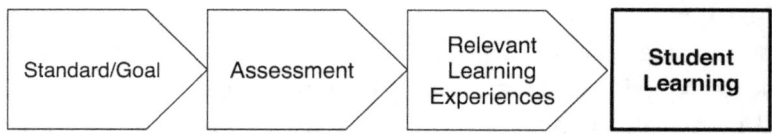

FIGURE 5.1 Stages of Backward Design

When Wiggins and McTighe (2005) introduced the concept of backward design, they changed the question from "What do I need to teach?" to "What do students need to know?" This reframing from a teacher-centered to a student-centered approach ensures alignment between learning standards, assessment, and classroom learning experiences, which promotes effective lesson planning.

If Monica had used a backward design approach, she likely would have focused more on the end goal of the unit and therefore would have been more strategic about which learning activities to include in her lesson. For example, on the first day of the unit, Monica wanted her students to be able to identify all the planets and state their order based on their distance from the sun. However, during the lesson, she brought up many other related topics, such as the consistency of the planets and space travel to the planets. While these topics are interesting and related to the lesson's goal, they do not support the desired outcome of the lesson taught that particular day and may confuse or overwhelm some students. Monica also had yet to consider how she would demonstrate their understanding of this standard, leaving her uncertain about moving forward in the unit. A simple exit ticket asking students to write down the planets in order of their distance from the sun would provide her with helpful data to inform her instructional decision-making for the next lesson. Table 5.1 provides the start of Monica's backward design, including the identification of a standard/goal and assessment, as she plans

TABLE 5.1 Backward Planning Lesson Example

Standard/Goal: *What will students know after this lesson?*	Students will be able to identify all planets and state their order based on distance from the sun.
Assessment: *How will you know students met the standard/goal?*	Students will complete an exit ticket marked 1-9. Students will start with the planet closest to the sun and then write down the planets in order from the sun.

her redo lesson. We will cover relevant learning experiences in the next section about explicit instruction.

Remember, using backward design means starting with the end in mind, identifying how to assess student learning, and planning the learning activities to get there. In the next section, we will discuss how to embed explicit instruction into relevant learning experiences so that your students can meet your set standards and goals.

Explicit Instruction

Explicit instruction is widely recognized for its positive impacts on student learning outcomes (Hughes et al., 2017). It has particularly benefited students with disabilities (Swanson et al., 2019) and multilingual learners (Baker et al., 2014). The use of explicit instruction has improved achievement across grade spans and subject areas (e.g., Hughes et al., 2017; Swanson et al., 2019; Vaughn & Fletcher, 2021). Highly esteemed educational agencies and organizations routinely advocate for explicit instruction in their guidance documents. For example, explicit instruction is included in numerous practice guides published by the What Works Clearinghouse (IES, n.d.). It is also identified as a high-leverage practice by the Council for Exceptional Children and the Collaboration for Effective Educator Development, Accountability and Reform (CEEDAR) Center (Aceves & Kennedy, 2024).

Explicit instruction (Archer & Hughes, 2011) is an instructional framework that identifies 16 research-based effective educator practices (see Table 5.2) in lesson development and delivery.

Educators skilled in explicit instruction will use some or all of the 16 elements within any lesson. To simplify the 16 elements of explicit instruction, educators often use the terms "Model, Lead, Test" or "I Do, We Do, You Do" to guide their planning. The big idea is to introduce new content by clearly identifying the goals for the lesson (also an essential first step in backward design planning), break up new content into manageable and meaningful chunks, teach the content by providing lots of modeling, including examples and non-examples, and opportunities for students to engage, strategically scaffold supports to promote independence, offer opportunities for guided practice and

TABLE 5.2 Elements of explicit instruction

1. Focus instruction on critical content.
2. Sequence skills logically.
3. Break down complex skills and strategies into smaller instructional units.
4. Design organized and focused lessons.
5. Begin lessons with a clear statement of the lesson's goals and your expectations.
6. Review prior skills and knowledge before beginning instruction.
7. Provide step-by-step demonstrations.
8. Use clear and concise language.
9. Provide an adequate range of examples and non-examples.
10. Provide guided and supported practice.
11. Require frequent responses.
12. Monitor student performance closely.
13. Provide immediate affirmative and corrective feedback.
14. Deliver the lesson at a brisk pace.
15. Help students organize knowledge.
16. Provide distributed and cumulative practice.

(Borrowed from Archer & Hughes, 2011)

progress monitoring with specific feedback, and then assess to check for understanding.

The research base behind explicit instruction provides educators with a range of strategies and educator behaviors to promote high rates of student achievement and engagement. When used consistently, explicit instruction can strengthen learning across curriculum areas, grade spans, and diverse student needs. Using what she learned about explicit instruction in her methods courses, Monica revamped her initial lesson to focus more intentionally on the lesson goal: Students will be able to identify all planets and state their order based on distance from the sun. Table 5.3 provides a glimpse into the explicit instruction section of her lesson plan.

Monica worked strategically to incorporate key components of explicit instruction into her lesson. She believed that this lesson would support learning for most of her students. However, she was still concerned about some of her students with unique needs. To ensure each and every one of her students could access the instruction and have their learning supported, Monica wanted to be sure she also incorporated UDL principles.

TABLE 5.3 Explicit Instruction: Body of Lesson

Hook: How will you get students interested in the topic?		Tell students the lesson's goal and then show a short National Geographic video that identifies the planets and discusses their order based on distance from the sun.
Explicit Instruction	**I Do:** Instruction and Modeling	Use labeled visuals to introduce each planet in order of their distance from the sun: (1) Mercury (2) Venus (3) Earth (4) Mars (5) Jupiter (6) Saturn (7) Uranus (8) Neptune. Demonstrate how to put the planets in order based on distance from the sun. Intentionally make errors, think aloud how the error was recognized, and correct the error. Use this to address any common misconceptions. Involve students through questioning throughout.
	We Do: Guided Practice	Show only one planet at a time. Scaffold for students by providing verbal prompts, hints, and intentional questions. Gradually fade prompts as you practice multiple times. 1. Ask students to call out, write, or sign the planet's name. 2. Ask students to identify the planet's place from the sun with their fingers or by holding up a number card. 3. Introduce ways to support memorization of the planet order. For example, offer multiple mnemonic devices to memorize. Invite students to create their own mnemonic device. Introduce a song to help students remember and sing together. 4. Practice using mnemonic devices and singing songs to name planets, allowing students to take more responsibility. Closely monitor performance of all students.
	You Do: Independent Practice	1. Once the students have demonstrated proficiency, they are ready to practice on their own. 2. Have students record themselves chanting the planets in order multiple times. Provide students 15 minutes to choose a method and practice independently.
Wrap Up: How will you summarize the information learned?		As a whole group, show visuals of the planets again. Use unlabeled versions and ask students to choral respond to each planet shown. The class works collectively to order the planets. Upon leaving, students will write, draw, or say the planets in order from the sun as an exit ticket.

Universal Design for Learning

In previous chapters, we discussed the breadth of diversity inherent in every classroom. Each student brings a range of unique personal characteristics, including their cultural/social identities, past learning experiences, dis/abilities, capacities, biology, cognitive abilities, and more. Educators are expected to ensure each of the roughly 20–30 students in a classroom have equitable access to instruction and positive outcomes. Is it any wonder that many educators find this challenging? Fortunately, if you embed the principles of the UDL framework into your lesson planning, you can address many students' needs (Hall et al., 2012).

No student should miss instruction due to an inability to engage, limited accessibility, or barriers to demonstrating their learning. As you start planning your lessons, use backward design planning to identify the lesson's goals, teach using explicit instruction principles, and ensure access for all by utilizing the UDL framework. The UDL framework recognizes, values, and proactively supports the expected variability within a student population (Hall et al., 2012). More often than not, educators plan a lesson and then consider what accommodations must occur to address student needs. Educators working from a UDL framework flip that thinking and instead plan for differentiation as a lesson is developed. Not only does this improve access, but it also enriches instruction. The UDL framework encourages educators to provide multiple means of engagement, representation, and action/expression (Meyer et al., 2017). Table 5.4 defines these three principles and offers some guiding questions for consideration.

Monica was happy with her new lesson plan as a starting point. However, knowing that some of her students had formal IEPs, 504 plans, and multilingual programming and others had informal needs, such as being an early finisher, having executive functioning challenges, and having sensory sensitivity, Monica wanted to be sure her lesson was accessible to the entire classroom community. After she designed her lesson, she referred to UDL principles to help her. Table 5.5 provides insight into her plan of action.

Monica verifies that her lesson plan generally matches UDL principles; and when she uncovers gaps by using UDL's guiding questions, she adjusts her lesson to effectively include the entire

TABLE 5.4 Principles of Universal Design for Learning

UDL Principle	Rationale	Guiding Questions
Provide multiple means of engagement	Individuals are sparked or motivated to learn for different reasons based on their unique characteristics.	Do students have opportunities to choose how they reach learning goals and demonstrate their learning? Are students with disabilities able to access the instruction? If not, how can barriers be removed?
Provide multiple means of representation	Students learn, generalize, and demonstrate acquired knowledge differently.	Do your students see themselves in the examples provided? Are lessons taught using varied sensory experiences, modalities, and forms of communication?
Provide multiple means of action and expression	Successfully engaging in learning activities will look and sound different for each student.	Are relevant learning activities varied enough so that all students can successfully navigate the tasks? Are students provided with varied tools to help them complete learning activities?

classroom community. Using the key principles of UDL to guide instructional decision-making allows the teacher to cast a wide net as they develop lessons and avoid focusing solely on the "average" student.

Classrooms are complex communities with many unique student characteristics requiring varying support and instructional practices. Planning effective instruction in an inclusive classroom requires more than content knowledge. Educators can use multiple lesson planning and instructional frameworks to promote positive student outcomes (Foxworth et al., 2022). Consider these key ideas:

- Know the intended outcomes of instruction and how students will demonstrate those outcomes by using a backward design model.
- Ensure instruction is clear, specific, engaging, and effective by incorporating explicit instruction elements.
- Support all students by embedding UDL principles within instruction.

TABLE 5.5 Universal Design for Learning Principles Lesson Planning Example

	Universal Design for Learning Considerations
How will you provide multiple means of engagement?	Students will have a choice of how they will learn and demonstrate their understanding of the planet order. Based on IEP, 504, and multilingual learner plans, relevant students will receive small group support throughout the lesson, especially during the guided practice section.
How will you provide multiple means of access?	Students will learn the order of the planets through multiple means, including: • Video—Visual/auditory • Lecture—Auditory • Choral responding—Oral • List/drawing—Written
How will you provide multiple means of action and expression?	Varied memorization techniques will be introduced. Students with executive functioning and sensory challenges will be offered only 2–3 memorization options based on their individual needs and preferences. When needed, they may focus on memorizing only the first four planets with a plan to continue with the remaining planets once they achieve fluency with the first 4.

Blending these concepts can help you to reach each student successfully. Table 5.6 offers research supporting the use of instructional frameworks as you plan instruction. A lesson plan template integrating backward design, explicit instruction, UDL principles, and positive behavior support practices from Chapter 4 is provided at the end of this chapter for your use (Appendix A). Additionally, we have provided a "Lesson Preparation" activity that can be paired with scripted lessons from curriculum manuals.

Key Takeaways

- *Effective lessons require comprehensive planning and preparation.*
- *Classroom communities are composed of many students with unique characteristics that need support.*
- *Using backward design, explicit instruction, and universal design for learning principles can support positive learning outcomes.*

TABLE 5.6 Research Highlighting the Efficacy of Instructional Frameworks

	What Does the Research Say?
Hughes et al., 2017	The following five key "pillars" or features of explicit instruction were determined based on a comprehensive review of explicit instruction components used in research studies that have shown efficacy. 1. Segment Complex Skills 2. Draw Student Attention to Important Features of the Content through Modeling/Think-Alouds 3. Promote Successful Engagement Using Systematically Faded Supports/Prompts 4. Provide Opportunities for Students to Respond and Receive Feedback 5. Create Purposeful Practice Opportunities These are not different than the original 16 elements. Instead, each pillar represents frequently used element(s).
King-Sears et al., 2023	A meta-analysis of 20 studies demonstrated that UDL-based instruction can bolster student achievement compared to non-UDL instruction.

Perspectives in Practice: A Mentor Teacher Guides Inclusive Lesson Planning

Ms. Brighton is a fourth-grade cooperating teacher. Her student teacher, Brittany, spent the first week of her placement familiarizing herself with the classroom routines, curricula, and students. Ms. Brighton gave Brittany the teacher's manual for the schoolwide reading curriculum used to provide universal reading instruction to all students. Brittany was amazed at the comprehensiveness and complexity of each lesson in the manual. She assumed that as long as she followed the directions for each lesson, she would be all set. Ms. Brighton smiled and said, "These lessons are developed for a classroom full of 'average students.' Following the lesson exactly as it is written in the manual won't cut it for the students in front of us." Ms. Brighton then provided a series of examples:

- ♦ Jakim will finish the assignment long before the others and will need an enrichment activity.
- ♦ There are too many questions for Susan to respond to all at once, which will make her agitated and could trigger

escalated behavior. She will need a modified version of the assignment.
- Raule is multilingual and cannot yet read English. He will need someone to read the directions to him and will write his responses in his native language.
- The content of the reading passage may be a trauma trigger for Isabella because her family experienced a home fire recently. Before you begin, she will need advanced notice.
- Malachi's IEP states that he needs multi-step directions broken down for him. As you give directions, remember to circle back and give him only one step at a time.

Brittany admitted that she had not considered how the needs of each individual student impacted her lesson planning process. She walked away from the meeting with many notes and some Post-Its on the manual pages to serve as prompts for when she delivers the lesson. She is grateful for her cooperating teacher's guidance and willingness to show her how to adapt the required curriculum to meet her students' needs.

Mentorship Corner: Supporting Effective Instructional Planning

Tips for Cooperating Teachers
- Before your student teacher begins lesson planning, spend time explaining and demonstrating your instructional decision-making process, including how you adapt or modify curricula (e.g., content, lessons within manuals) to meet the diverse needs of your student population. As your student teacher begins to take on lesson planning and delivery, provide scaffolded support until their confidence and competence strengthen.
- Use the 5-15-45 Minute Tool[1] from the TIES Center with your student teacher to help identify and find solutions to barriers to student instruction.

Tips for University Supervisors

- ♦ Offer lesson plan templates (such as the examples within this chapter) that prompt critical elements such as engagement strategies, prompts, differentiation opportunities, accommodations, and modification needs.
- ♦ With each new area, student teachers begin to teach, ask for lesson plans ahead of time, and provide feedback.
- ♦ As student teachers take on instructional lesson planning in new areas, ask them to bring in their lesson plans to share in small groups. Use the small group process to brainstorm potential barriers to access and accompanying solutions.

Practice and Reflect: Application Activities to Support Your Development

In Your Classroom

- At the beginning of your placement, ask your cooperating teacher for a class list and access to students' IEP, 504, multilingual learner, MTSS, and other support plans. Create a comprehensive chart of accommodations, modifications, and supports to review as you plan lessons and related learning activities.

In Seminar

- Share a lesson plan for an upcoming lesson and, in small groups, brainstorm enhancements and ask for specific feedback prior to implementation.

On Your Own

- Following each lesson, take a moment to reflect and consider the following questions:
  - Did all students achieve the goals of the lesson?
  - Was the instruction clear and engaging?
  - What got in the way of the students who could have been more successful?

Teacher Toolbox: Resources for Further Exploration

1. This video[2] provides an explanation of Backward Design as a planning framework.
2. The following High Leverage Practices for Inclusive Classrooms (highleveragepractices.org)[3] videos demonstrate some key practices mentioned in this chapter.
    - HLP 11: Identify and prioritize long- and short-term learning goals.[4]
    - HLP 12: Systematically design instruction toward a specific learning goal.[5]
    - HLP 15: Provide scaffolded supports.[6]
    - HLP 16: Use explicit instruction.[7]
3. Videos of explicit instruction in action can be found at explicitinstruction.org.[8]
4. The National Center for Intensive Intervention offers free explicit instruction course modules.[9]
5. The Center for Applied Special Technology (CAST) offers Universal Design for Learning (UDL) Guidelines and resources[10] to support implementation of the guidelines.
6. The Iris Center provides a self-paced Universal Design for Learning[11] module.

Notes

1. https://publications.ici.umn.edu/ties/5-15-45/overview
2. https://youtu.be/4isSHf3SBuQ
3. https://highleveragepractices.org/
4. https://highleveragepractices.org/hlp-11-goal-setting
5. https://highleveragepractices.org/hlp-12-systematically-design-instruction-toward-specific-learning-goal?_gl=1*1duf6io*_ga*OTk3MDQyMjE0LjE3MTgyMDQyNjU.*_ga_L4ZFTNESGT*MTcxOTUxNTc2My42LjEuMTcxOTUxNjgwMS4zMS4wLjA.
6. https://highleveragepractices.org/hlp-15-use-scaffolded-supports
7. https://highleveragepractices.org/hlp-16-use-explicit-instruction?_gl=1*ki79q8*_ga*OTk3MDQyMjE0LjE3MTgyMDQyNjU.*_ga_L4ZFTNESGT*MTcxOTUxNTc2My42LjEuMTcxOTUxNjk4OC4zMC4wLjA.

8. http://explicitinstruction.org/
9. https://intensiveintervention.org/training/course-content/explicit-instruction
10. https://udlguidelines.cast.org/
11. https://iris.peabody.vanderbilt.edu/module/udl/

References

Aceves, T. C., & Kennedy, M. J. (2024). High-leverage practices for students with disabilities.

Archer, A. L., & Hughes, C. A. (2011). *Explicit instruction: Effective and efficient teaching*. Guilford Publications.

Baker, S., Lesaux, N., Jayanthi, M., Dimino, J., Proctor, C. P., & Morris, J. et al. (2014). *Teaching academic content and literacy to English learners in elementary and middle school* (NCEE 2014–4012). National Center for Education Evaluation and Regional Assistance (NCEE), Institute of Education Sciences, U.S. Department of Education. Retrieved from: https://ies.ed.gov/ncee/wwc/PracticeGuides

Foxworth, L. L., Hashey, A. I., Dexter, C., Rasnitsyn, S., & Beck, R. (2022). Approaching explicit instruction within a universal design for learning framework. *Teaching Exceptional Children*, *54*(4), 268–275. https://doi.org/10.1177/00400599211010190

Hall, T. E., Meyer, A., & Rose, D. H. (2012). *Universal design for learning in the classroom*. Guilford Press.

Hughes, C. A., Morris, J. R., Therrien, W. J., & Benson, S. K. (2017). Explicit instruction: Historical and contemporary contexts. *Learning Disabilities Research & Practice*, *32*(3), 140–148. https://doi.org/10.1111/ldrp.12142

Institute of Education Sciences. (n.d.). *Practice Guides*. https://ies.ed.gov/ncee/wwc/PracticeGuides

King-Sears, M. E., Stefanidis, A., Evmenova, A. S., Rao, K., Mergen, R. L., Owen, L. S., & Strimel, M. M. (2023). Achievement of learners receiving UDL instruction: A meta-analysis, *Teaching and Teacher Education*, *122*, 103956. https://doi.org/10.1016/j.tate.2022.103956

Meyer, A., Rose, D. H., Gordon, D., Riccomini, P. J., Morano, S., & Hughes, C. A. (2017). Big ideas in special education: Specially designed instruction, high-leverage practices, explicit instruction, and intensive instruction. *Teaching Exceptional Children*, *50*(1), 20–27. https://doi.org/10.1177/0040059917724412

Swanson, E., Stevens, E. A., & Wexler, J. (2019). Engaging students with disabilities in text-based discussions: Guidance for general education social studies classrooms. *Teaching Exceptional Children*, *51*(4), 305–312. https://doi.org/10.1177/0040059919826030

Vaughn, S., & Fletcher, J. (2021). Explicit instruction as the essential tool for executing the science of reading. *The Reading League Journal*, *2*(2), 4–11.

Wiggins, G. P., & McTighe, J. (2005). *Understanding by design*. ASCD.

APPENDIX A: LESSON PLAN TEMPLATE

Date:		Subject:	
Standard/Goal: *What will students know after this lesson?*			
Assessment: *How will you know students met the standard/goal?*			
Materials Needed:			

Brainstorm 3–5 possible specific praise statements to use in this lesson:

What prompts need to be provided throughout the lesson?

What OTRs will you use in each section of the lesson?

Hook: *How will you get students interested in the topic?*			

Explicit Instruction	**I Do:** *Instruction and Modeling*		
	We Do: *Guided Practice*		
	You Do: *Independent Practice*		
Wrap-Up: *How will you summarize the information learned?*			
Universal Design for Learning Considerations:			
How will you provide multiple means of engagement?			
How will you provide multiple means of access?			
How will you provide multiple means of action and expression?			
Pre-reflection (if using for student teaching observation): What background information would you like me to know about your class and/or today's lesson? Is there anything specific that you would like me to observe?			

APPENDIX B: LESSON PREPARATION TEMPLATE (FOR SCRIPTED LESSONS)

Directions: This lesson preparation activity can be used **in lieu of creating a lesson plan** when you are preparing to teach a direct instruction lesson from **a scripted or curriculum guide**. The following steps can be taken to ensure that you are well-prepared to deliver your lesson at an appropriate pace and that your delivery is interactive and includes appropriate monitoring, feedback, and practice.

Grade level standard:	
Specific skill(s) addressed:	

Curriculum resource:		
Initial preparation activities	Check	Activity
		Read through entire lesson.
		Practice delivering the entire lesson.
		Add prompts (e.g., sticky notes, visual cues) to support effective delivery.

Delivering Instruction and Active Participation:

1. Do I need to review any pre-requisite skills?
2. How will I provide appropriate models?
3. What questions will I ask students in order to monitor progress?
4. How will I elicit responses to make the lesson interactive for *all* students?
5. What scaffolds will I use to guide student understanding?
6. How will I provide feedback throughout the lesson?

Classroom Management Considerations:

1. What prompt/pre-correction will I provide at the start of the lesson to remind students about any behavioral expectations?
2. How will I reinforce desired behavior?
3. Are there any anticipated behavioral concerns, and how can I be proactive in setting up students for success?

Student Considerations:

1. How can I incorporate the UDL framework?
2. What individual student accommodations should I consider?

Formal Observations Pre-Reflection (if using for student teaching observation):

1. What specific practices would you like me to watch for today?
2. Is there any background information that would provide context for this observation?

6

Instructional Delivery and Engagement in the Inclusive Classroom

Samantha is working toward a secondary math certification, and she's currently a student teacher at the high school level. After assuming full responsibility for teaching the Algebra I class a week ago, she gave her students a quiz, and she was disappointed with their performance. During instruction, it appeared that her students were quietly following along. When she asked if they understood the content, they nodded affirmatively. When she asked them questions, they seemed to get the answers right. So, Samantha is wondering, what happened? Samantha's university supervisor recommends that she record and then watch her next lesson to get a better feel for what her students are doing when she is teaching. When she watches the video, she notices that each time she asks a question during instruction to monitor student understanding, the same 3 students out of 25 raise their hands. She realizes the majority of the students never participate and, while she assumed everyone was understanding, it may have only been a small group. Samantha sits down with her cooperating teacher to discuss strategies for increasing student engagement that will allow her to monitor the performance of all students, not just the performance of the few who are the most willing.

In Chapter 5, we were introduced to elements of effective planning including backwards design, explicit instruction, and universal design for learning. A solid lesson plan provides a strong foundation for delivering a fantastic lesson that helps your students to think critically, gain knowledge and skills, and make connections to themselves and the world around them. With a good plan in place, it's time to think about how you can best deliver it. In this chapter, we will look closely at elements of effective delivery, including techniques to increase student engagement, monitor student progress, provide appropriate feedback, and adjust instruction as needed. Lesson delivery is challenging for the novice teacher because of the "high cognitive load" of the work; in other words, as a new teacher, you are just getting comfortable with the content, figuring out classroom management, responding to the unexpected, battling nerves, and this is all new! So, give yourself some time to develop your skills in this area over the course of student teaching. When delivery feels "off," simply use it as an opportunity to grow. With the support of your cooperating teacher and university supervisor, delivering effective instruction in the inclusive classroom will be an area of tremendous growth for you.

Instructional Delivery

Setting the Stage

Think back for a moment to your own school experiences. Can you remember sitting in a class and feeling too scared to raise your hand or, worse yet, feeling terrified that the teacher would "cold-call" on you? On the other hand, perhaps you can remember a time when you felt confident to answer a question, or share your ideas without fear of being "wrong?" Before we dive into strategies to increase student engagement, let's discuss how we can set up an environment where students feel comfortable actively participating, collaborating, responding to instruction, and asking questions.

In Chapter 3, *The Classroom Environment*, we discussed practices for setting up a positive, productive environment that is culturally responsive and conducive to learning. Using the practices outlined in Chapter 3 will provide a strong foundation for creating a safe environment where all students feel comfortable actively participating. In Table 6.1, we provide examples of how these practices can be used to support student engagement and active participation. Use these practices to create a classroom environment that encourages rather than discourages active participation among all students in the inclusive classroom. Additionally, always be mindful of peer relationships among your students, and reinforce students for being kind and inclusive.

Active Participation

When students are engaged in classroom learning activities, we see positive results for both behavior and academic performance. The good news is that there is a lot that we can do as teachers to help our students to be actively engaged—even those who are the most reluctant (MacSuga-Gage & Simonsen, 2015). Research shows that providing students with high rates of high-quality teacher-delivered opportunities to respond (OTR) can lead to gains in achievement and a reduction in problem behaviors. In the inclusive classroom, varying the types of OTRs is a useful strategy for engaging students with disabilities and other diverse needs, as well as those who may feel more reluctant to participate for a variety of reasons. While it is very important to consider when and what type of OTRs you will use during the lesson planning process, a skilled teacher can make decisions about using OTRs throughout instructional delivery. With practice, you will soon be able to do this, too!

Table 6.2 provides examples of various OTR types. Ideally, you want to think about how you can maximize student responding for all students. While it is perfectly fine to use individual questioning, as Samantha was using at the start of this chapter, it is important to recognize that this type of OTR limits engagement across the whole class and may give you a false sense of student understanding. There are more effective ways to elicit responses from all or at least most students. Using a wide variety of OTR types frequently will maximize learning for

TABLE 6.1 Establishing a Safe Environment for Active Participation

	Description	Example
Explicitly teach expectations	Develop expectations for participation during various activities. Teach students how to participate appropriately in specific contexts.	Jane, a high school ELA student teacher, explicitly teaches an expectation for active participation in collaborative groups. Students rotate specific roles (e.g., leader, notetaker, researcher, reporter), and Jane models each job, as well as other behaviors that support collaboration among group members (e.g., taking turns, active listening, questioning).
Provide prompts	Prior to various activities, provide reminders to encourage participation. Pre-correct any student behaviors that could interfere with participation.	Prior to beginning a direct instruction lesson in his first-grade phonics activity, Ryan tells students that he will be listening closely for all voices during a choral responding activity.
Specific praise	Reinforce active and appropriate participation. Consider your positive-to-negative feedback ratio.	After prompting her students to discuss a question with a partner, Maya praises her middle school social studies class: "I was just listening in on conversations and everyone was engaged and on topic!"
Active supervision	Move around the room throughout direct instruction and collaborative group activities.	During collaborative group work in his fourth-grade class, Hasan frequently moves around the room and reinforces active participation among students.
Acknowledgment systems	Consider how you can encourage active participation in a class-wide acknowledgment system.	MaryBeth uses an interdependent group contingency in her elementary music class. When all kids participate in singing their newly learned song, she adds a token to their class jar. Her class has already selected the musical they want to watch once it's filled up.

TABLE 6.2 Opportunities to Respond Examples

	Strategy in Action
Verbal	**Choral responding:** All students respond to a question at the same time. Most useful for short responses with only one correct answer. It is important to teach a choral responding procedure (e.g., establish a signal that you will give when it is appropriate to respond). **Think-pair-share:** Ask a question, allow for "think" time, ask students to pair with a friend to discuss responses, and, finally, call on several students to share with the whole class. It is important to actively supervise discussions so that you can monitor understanding. You can also consider adding a writing component where students write down answers before they pair. **Close reading:** Read a passage aloud to students and ask them to follow along. Pause at specific words that you want students to read aloud in unison.
Non-verbal	**Response cards:** Give your students a set of pre-made cards or have them make their own cards. Cards can reflect common responses such as yes/no or true/false, or they can be content-specific (such as a vocabulary review), which may require multiple-choice responses. Ask questions, give wait time, and then prompt students to hold up the correct answer. This is a helpful strategy when the number of responses is limited. **White boards:** Each student or pair of students receives a small white board, marker, and eraser. Students write responses to your questions on their white boards. Prompt the students to hold up responses. This is a useful strategy when the responses are longer, varied, or based on opinion. **Action responses:** There are many ways that you can ask students to respond to a question or request with an action. Pointing, using hand signals, acting out, or moving to a spot in the room are examples of action responses. **Guided notes:** Provide students with an outline of content to be discussed in class. Leave blanks for students to fill in as you are sharing your lecture or having a discussion. This is useful for helping all students to keep pace.

your students. Research shows that good teachers provide 3–5 OTRs per minute for simple responses (e.g., choral responding, response cards). More complex OTRs, such as collaborative group work, require more time (Haydon et al., 2012). Table 6.3 offers further insight into the research on active participation.

TABLE 6.3 Research on Active Engagement Strategies

	What Does the Research Say?
Research Study	*Key Takeaway*
MacSuga-Gage & Simonsen, 2015	This review of the literature provides support for previous research showing that when teachers provide students with more opportunities to respond (OTRs) to instruction, we see improvements in both academic and behavioral outcomes.
Duchaine et al., 2018	This study compared participation rates and academic achievement between response cards and traditional hand raising for students with disabilities in inclusive classrooms. Both participation and achievement improved with response cards.
Konrad et al., 2011	The results of this meta-analysis provide support for using guided notes as a strategy to promote active engagement, teach note-taking skills, and improve academic achievement.

Key Takeaways

- *A good lesson plan provides a strong foundation for a well-delivered lesson, and student teaching provides an opportunity to practice and improve your delivery skills continually.*
- *Your students are more likely to participate when they feel safe, comfortable, and confident. Using specific strategies, such as prompting and specific praise, with a focus on engagement can help.*
- *Using a variety of opportunities to respond will help to improve participation from all students in your inclusive classroom.*

Teaching Practices in the Inclusive Classroom

Giving and Receiving Feedback

Using a variety of OTRs will ideally provide you with an opportunity to monitor student understanding and progress throughout your lesson delivery. As students are responding, it is important to listen carefully, scan, and walk around the room, and communicate (Archer & Hughes, 2010). This type of ongoing, informal assessment used to monitor progress falls under the umbrella of "formative," and research has shown that formative assessment significantly contributes to learning (Kirschner & Hendrick, 2020). Why? Simply put, assessment that can be used to help us determine next steps is a powerful tool because it allows us to make necessary adjustments. OTRs provide you with feedback. Do your students understand the content? Are there misunderstandings that need to be addressed? Are there gaps in knowledge or skills that need to be filled before moving on? These are essential questions to be asking yourself in the inclusive classroom. Formative assessment allows you to confirm student understanding and progress toward learning objectives, and it provides feedback to indicate when additional review is needed.

Providing quality feedback to your students based on their responses is critical to their success. However, it is important to note that not all feedback is created equal. Feedback that is too general can not only be useless, but it may also put more pressure on students who are already confused; moreover, when there are knowledge gaps, sometimes it is more instruction that is needed rather than feedback. In their paper "The Power of Feedback," researchers Hattie and Timperley (2007) share three major questions we can ask ourselves when considering feedback: Where am I going? (What are the lesson goals?); How am I going? (Are all students making progress toward goals?); and Where to next? (What activities are needed for better progress?). Feedback that is immediate, context-specific, informative, non-threatening to student confidence, focused on the task and how students can improve, and goal-oriented will be most beneficial for student learning (Hattie & Timperley, 2007). Archer and Hughes (2010) suggest asking yourself the following questions as you consider the type of feedback needed to help students reach learning goals (Table 6.4):

Is each response correct?
If the response is correct, what type of affirmation is best?
If the response is incorrect, what type of correction procedure should be used?

TABLE 6.4 Affirmative and Corrective Feedback (Archer & Hughes, 2010)

Teacher Question/Request	Student Response	Example Feedback	Rationale
A Kindergarten teacher asks students to choral respond to the question: "What day of the week comes after Tuesday?"	After giving the choral response signal, all students confidently reply "Wednesday!" in unison.	The teacher says, "that's right!" and moves on to the next question.	When responses are correct and students are confident, a quick acknowledgment that the answer is correct prior to moving on helps to maintain a brisk pace.
A middle school teacher asks her students to work with a partner to list the steps of the scientific method.	While the final answers are correct, the teacher notices hesitancy and a lack of confidence as pairs try to complete lists.	The teacher tells students that the answers are correct but reviews the procedure to scaffold support and build confidence.	When responses are correct, but students lack confidence, are hesitant, or appear to be guessing, it is important to repeat and/or review.
A fifth-grade teacher asks her students to point to the Nile River in Africa on their maps.	Many students incorrectly point to the Congo River in Africa.	The teacher points to the Nile River on the classroom world map and asks students to find the correct river on their own maps.	When students make knowledge-based errors, teachers can simply state the fact and have students repeat the information.
A high school Algebra I teacher asks her students to use the order of operations to solve an equation on a worksheet.	As the teacher walks around the room, they notice that many students are not correctly applying the strategy, which leads to incorrect answers.	The teacher reteaches how to apply the order of operations when solving equations, involving students in the process.	When students make errors applying strategies or using procedures, involve them in the reteaching and then have them practice to confirm understanding.

What adaptations to the current lesson are needed?
Do I need to reteach facts, concepts, skills, or strategies immediately or in a future lesson?
Do I need to provide additional practice now or in a future lesson?

Scaffolding

It is likely that you are already familiar with the term "scaffolding," a practice we refer to in Chapter 5 when discussing elements of Explicit Instruction and the "I Do, We Do, You, Do" model. When delivering instruction, appropriately scaffolding learning is critically important, yet it is tricky to get it just right. So, what exactly does good scaffolding look like in practice? To answer this question, let's first return to our example about learning how to drive in order to look at effective scaffolding in a different context. Perhaps you remember the first few times you were behind the wheel and on the road with an instructor (professional or family member) in the passenger's seat. In these initial days and weeks of learning to apply the rules of the road to practice, it is likely that your instructor provided you with a great deal of guidance, including prompts, reminders, and specific feedback about how things went. Over time, as you began to demonstrate proficiency and gain confidence in your skills, your instructor likely provided less and less guidance, leaving you with greater and greater responsibility until you were finally able to drive independently. This is scaffolding in action—the fading of instructor guidance, including prompts, reminders, questions, and feedback, until the learner is independent.

In the classroom setting, scaffolding requires empathy and patience from the teacher so that student frustration can be minimized. Finding the right "not too easy or difficult" spot—or what is sometimes referred to as the *Zone of Proximal Development* (Vygotsky, 1978)—is a challenging task for all teachers, especially those with less experience. As you work to enhance your delivery skills during student teaching, practice scaffolding by providing prompts, offering hints, and asking questions as your students progress from one skill to the next, and remember to fade these supports as students demonstrate proficiency

(Kirschner & Hendrick, 2020). With this focus, you will become more and more confident in differentiating and responding to student needs during instruction.

Pacing

Providing students with just the right amount of time to think, learn, make connections, respond to requests, and complete tasks is no easy feat for any teacher, and pacing your lesson delivery will be an area to focus on throughout the student teaching semester. Giving students too much time can result in off-task, and sometimes contextually inappropriate, behavior, as well as lost learning time. Giving students too little time can lead to frustration and can interfere with learning. Finding out what "just the right amount" of time is for your students is difficult, and it can vary from one group of students to the next and from student to student. We recommend planning out the pace of your lesson prior to delivery. You can do this by breaking your lesson into sections and allocating estimated time for each one.

Two additional areas for consideration are providing "think time" and keeping a brisk pace. When you ask a question, give your students time to think quietly, and then cue them to respond. This is very helpful when providing whole-class OTRs. Without adequate think time, your quickest responders might blurt out the answers while other students mentally check-out. It can be helpful to ask your students to give you a sign when they have a response (e.g., "put your hand on your head when you have an opinion to share"). This technique also provides students with some accountability for doing the thinking—an activity that we obviously cannot see happening.

Keeping a brisk pace is also important for good pacing of instructional delivery (Archer & Hughes, 2010). With active supervision and progress monitoring, you can listen carefully for cues that let you know it is time to move on. For example, when asking students to think-pair-share, be sure to circulate when students are in paired discussions. Listen closely to conversations to monitor discussions and, as conversations begin to wind down, prompt students to begin wrapping up and remind them that they will soon be asked to share with the class. During the share time, you do not need to hear from every pair; one or two students sharing out to the whole class will help you to stay on track and move the lesson forward.

Observation and Reflection

Observation and self-reflection are critical components of any teacher's professional development and are key to helping you develop your instructional delivery skills. See Table 6.5 for research on improving teacher practices. Your classroom cooperating teacher will make observations informally on a regular basis, and it is important to set aside time for more formal observations that are focused on developing specific instructional skills. Both your cooperating teacher and university supervisor play a crucial role in providing objective, constructive feedback following observations. You might consider asking them to watch for specific practices you are working to improve, or to collect data on your use of important teaching practices, such as your use of OTRs. In addition to asking your mentors what can be done to improve your delivery skills, be sure to ask for some reinforcement about what is going well and what has improved over time. Keep in mind that constructive feedback is meant to be helpful, not hurtful. While it can sometimes feel like you did something "wrong" when a mentor shares ideas for improvement, the intention is to help you grow and be ready for your own classroom. If feedback ever feels critical, vague, or confusing, be sure to ask for clarification.

TABLE 6.5 Research on Strategies to Improve Teacher Practice

	What Does the Research Say?
Research Study	Key Takeaway
McKellar et al., 2020	Using the Classroom Assessment Learning System, researchers examined 11 dimensions of specific teaching practices and found that quality feedback was the strongest predictor of students' active engagement. Quality feedback is defined as use of feedback loops, encouragement of responses, and explanation of performance.
Nagro et al., 2017	This study examined the effects of guided video analysis on pre-service teachers' instructional skills and self-reflection. Pre-service teachers who video-recorded their instruction and wrote reflections four times during student teaching showed significant improvements in instructional skills over time.

In addition to informal and formal mentor observations, video self-observation provides a valuable opportunity for reflection, growth, and improvement. As a student teacher, you will have a lot on your mind while you deliver lessons. Recording your teaching and watching it back later can provide you with an opportunity to see the classroom from a completely different vantage point. Research has shown that collecting data through video self-analysis is an effective way to enhance use of targeted delivery skills, such as behavior-specific praise (VanLone et al., 2022). Consider watching your video alongside your cooperating teacher or university supervisor, and take time to pause and discuss aspects of your instruction. We include a useful tool to help guide your reflection, *The Classroom Practices Video Self-Analysis Tool*, at the end of this chapter (Appendix C).

Equally important to frequent observations is setting aside time for self-reflection. Good teaching requires humility, vulnerability, and deep, honest reflection. Recognizing our strengths and successes can help you to maintain a sense of joy and appreciation for this work. Noting challenges and areas in which you can improve can help you to set goals and implement changes to your practice. Key questions to consider during self-reflection might include: "What aspects of the lesson delivery went well, and why?"; "Which students met the learning objectives today, and were there students who needed more support?"; "What strategies did I use to actively engage students, and were all students engaged throughout the lesson?"; and "What specific steps can I take to improve my practice moving forward?" By critically analyzing your instructional delivery and considering these questions, you can develop a reflective mindset that will support continuous growth throughout your teaching career.

Key Takeaways

- *Providing your students with varied and high rates of OTRs will help you to monitor their understanding and to provide targeted, constructive feedback.*
- *Scaffolding is a form of differentiation in the inclusive classroom. Gradually pulling back supports such as verbal and*

visual prompts and guided questioning while your students assume more responsibility and gain confidence is a highly effective delivery method.
♦ *Formal, informal, and self-observations paired with reflection can help you to develop critical teaching skills throughout your student teaching experience (and your entire teaching career).*

Perspectives in Practice: Developing Self-Reflection through Journaling

Lee stood at the front of the classroom, her heart still racing from the lesson she had just delivered. The students had filed out a few minutes ago, leaving the room in a quiet lull. The sound of the clock ticking seemed to grow louder as she replayed the supervisor's feedback in her mind. "You've got a lot of potential, Lee," her student teaching supervisor had said earlier that day. "But I'd like you to focus on a few key areas: instructional delivery, student engagement, and feedback." Lee took out her journal. She'd always found writing to be a helpful way to process her thoughts. Today, though, she wasn't sure where to begin. She knew her supervisor's feedback was meant to help her grow, but the specifics felt daunting. She needed a plan—something concrete to work on—so she started jotting down questions.

1. What is my current approach to instructional delivery?

    Lee thought back to her lesson. She'd followed the lesson plan closely, making sure to cover each point she had prepared. But was that enough? She realized she often focused so much on getting through the material that she might not be considering how she was delivering it. Was she varying her tone, using body language effectively, or checking for understanding throughout the lesson?

2. How can I make my instructional delivery more engaging?

    This question felt broad, but it was important. Lee had noticed a few students zoning out during her lesson, their eyes glazed over as she talked. How could she pull them back in? Maybe she could incorporate more interactive activities to break up the lecture. She also thought about her pacing—was she moving too quickly or too slowly? Would more pauses give students time to process the information? Perhaps she could start asking more open-ended questions to involve students in the discussion.

3. How am I engaging my students, and how can I improve?

Lee had always seen herself as someone who could connect well with people, but the classroom was different from one-on-one interactions. She remembered her supervisor mentioning that some students seemed disengaged. Maybe she needed to be more mindful of how she called on students—making sure to include everyone and not just the ones who always raised their hands. She also considered incorporating more varied OTRs throughout her lessons to help.

4. What kind of feedback am I giving my students?

Lee knew that feedback was essential for student growth, but she wasn't sure if she was providing it effectively. Was she giving feedback that was specific and actionable? Did her students know what they were doing well and what they needed to work on? She decided she would try to incorporate more formative assessments into her lessons so she could give immediate, targeted feedback.

5. How can I measure my progress?

It was easy to set goals, but Lee knew it was just as important to find ways to measure her progress. She decided to ask her supervisor if she could be observed again in a few weeks, with specific focus areas in mind.

With these questions guiding her, Lee began to draft a plan. She listed out specific strategies she could implement in her next lesson, such as using more visuals, incorporating think-pair-share activities, and preparing a set of formative questions to check for understanding. She also set a reminder to record herself teaching so she could review her delivery and reflect on her progress. After all, teaching is not just delivering content—it is about growing, adapting, and constantly striving to do better. And Lee was ready to do just that.

Mentorship Corner: Supporting Effective Delivery

Tips for Cooperating Teachers

- Use a variety of OTRs during your own instruction to model effective delivery. Share your rationale for using specific strategies to engage all students throughout your lessons. When you are modeling, ask your student teacher to watch for specific OTRs and how they might affect engagement. Discuss your decision-making process for providing specific feedback based on their performance.
- Scaffold support for your student teacher's use of effective delivery skills throughout the semester. Consider this example:
    - *Early semester*: Share your lesson plans with your student teacher and explain how you plan to use specific strategies to increase student engagement, monitor learning, and provide feedback. Ask your student teacher to watch for these delivery elements when observing you. Model good self-reflection following informal observations, sharing what you think went well and what could be improved. Ask for your student teacher's feedback.
    - *Mid-semester*: Meet with your student teacher to discuss their lesson plans. Provide feedback on their plans for using effective delivery elements. Encourage them to incorporate a variety of strategies. Discuss potential issues that may arise with student progress and explore how specific feedback might be used to scaffold support throughout instruction. Provide targeted feedback for your student teacher's use of delivery strategies.
    - *Late-semester*: Record your student teacher delivering instruction. Watch the video together and help your

student teacher to self-reflect on delivery by asking guided questions.

Tips for University Supervisors

♦ Check for any gaps in understanding regarding delivery skills. Do your student teachers understand the rationale for using these strategies? Do you understand the connection between OTRs, formative assessment, specific feedback, and student achievement?
♦ During formal observations, provide feedback to your student teachers on their use of delivery strategies. Consider collecting data on use of OTRs and recording instances of feedback delivered to correct and incorrect responses. When working on pacing, consider "time-stamping" throughout the observation.
♦ Share successes and provide effective feedback during post-observations. Guide self-reflection using questioning and help your student teachers to identify targeted goals. Develop a plan for making small improvements.

Practice and Reflect: Application Activities to Support Your Development

---

In Your Classroom

- Once you have created your lesson plans, set aside time for lesson rehearsal. You can rehearse key parts of a lesson with your cooperating teacher and receive feedback on pacing and ideas for scaffolding and engagement.

In Seminar or Post-observation Meetings

- Arrange in-person observations with willing members of your cohort. Provide feedback on your peers' use of student engagement and feedback in post-observation meetings.

On Your Own

- Use video self-analysis to observe and reflect on your own performance. At the end of this chapter, we include a video self-analysis tool to help you reflect on instructional delivery and classroom management.

Teacher Toolbox: Resources for Further Exploration

1. *High Leverage Practices for Inclusive Classrooms* (highleveragepractices.org)[1]: Watch HLP #18 "Use strategies to promote active student engagement" and HLP #22 "Provide positive and constructive feedback to guide students' learning and behavior."
2. *The Teaching Channel*: New Teacher Survival Guide: The Formal Observation.[2] (Requires subscription.)
3. *GoReact*:[3] Observation tool for teacher candidates that allows supervisors to provide time-stamped feedback throughout a video recording of teaching. (Requires subscription.) See sample GoReact assignment in Appendix A.
4. *Mursion*:[4] Virtual training simulations for pre-service teachers. (Requires subscription.)
5. Classroom Analysis Activity: Pre-service teachers can use this tool to help focus on instructional delivery when observing their cooperating teacher. See attached assignment in Appendix B.
6. *Classroom Practices Video Self-Analysis Guided Reflection Tool*: See attached sample assignment in Appendix C.

Notes

1. https://highleveragepractices.org/.
2. https://learn.teachingchannel.com/video/preparing-for-formal-observations.
3. https://get.goreact.com/teacher-education/.
4. https://www.mursion.com/services/education/.

References

Archer, A. L., & Hughes, C. A. (2010). *Explicit instruction: Effective and efficient teaching*. Guilford Publications.

Duchaine, E. L., Jolivette, K., Fredrick, L. D., & Alberto, P. A. (2018). Increase engagement and achievement with response cards: Science and mathematics inclusion classes. *Learning Disabilities: A Contemporary Journal*, *16*(2), 157. https://link.gale.com/apps/doc/A561522153/AONE?u=bucknell_it&sid=bookmark-AONE&xid=2da013aa

Hattie, J., & Timperley, H. (2007). The power of feedback. *Review of Educational Research*, *77*(1), 81–112. https://doi.org/10.3102/003465430298487

Haydon, T., Macsuga-Gage, A. S., Simonsen, B., & Hawkins, R. (2012). Opportunities to respond: A key component of effective instruction. *Beyond Behavior*, *22*(1), 23–31. https://doi.org/10.1177/107429561202200105

Kirschner, P. A., & Hendrick, C. (2020). *How learning happens: Seminal works in educational psychology and what they mean in practice*. Routledge.

Konrad, M., Joseph, L. M., & Itoi, M. (2011). Using guided notes to enhance instruction for all students. *Intervention in School and Clinic*, *46*(3), 131–140. https://doi.org/10.1177/1053451210378163

MacSuga-Gage, A. S., & Simonsen, B. (2015). Examining the effects of teacher-directed opportunities to respond on student outcomes: A systematic review of the literature. *Education and Treatment of Children*, *38*(2), 211–239. http://www.jstor.org/stable/44683954

McKellar, S. E., Cortina, K. S., & Ryan, A. M. (2020). Teaching practices and student engagement in early adolescence: A longitudinal study using the classroom assessment scoring system. *Teaching and Teacher Education*, *89*, 102936.

Nagro, S. A., deBettencourt, L. U., Rosenberg, M. S., Carran, D. T., & Weiss, M. P. (2017). The effects of guided video analysis on teacher Candidates' reflective ability and instructional skills. *Teacher Education and Special Education*, *40*(1), 7–25. https://doi.org/10.1177/0888406416680469

VanLone, J., Freeman, J., Simonsen, B., Everett, S., Sugai, G., & Whitcomb, S. (2022). The effects of a video self-analysis package on pre-service Teachers' use of behavior-specific praise. *The Journal of Special Education Apprenticeship*, *11*(1). https://doi.org/10.58729/2167-3454.1131

Vygotsky, L. S. (1978). *Mind in society: The development of higher psychological processes*. Harvard University Press.

APPENDIX A: GoReact SAMPLE ASSIGNMENT

Recording Directions: Download the GoReact app and log in to your account. Locate Assignment 1. Please record approximately 20–30 minutes of your classroom instruction. Note that there is a 30-minute time limit on recordings. This does not mean that you need to squeeze your entire lesson into 30 minutes.

Assignment Directions: Watch your video. As you watch, use the following markers to "tag" specific instances of your behaviors. You do not need to tag every single instance of a teacher behavior; simply record when you notice that you did use them **or that you could have used them.** Tag/reflect at least 10 times.

Tags for This Assignment

AS: Active Supervision: use this marker when you are walking around the room to supervise and check-in with students and monitor progress.

FB: Feedback: use this marker when you provide specific feedback (behavior-specific praise, for example).

SF: Use this marker when you scaffold support for students.

OV: Opportunity to respond (varied): use this when you ask more than one student to respond.

O1: Opportunity to respond 1-1: use this when you ask one student to respond.

Self-Reflection

In addition to using the markers, you can type in the comment box. Please type at least five reflection comments in your video.

You can reflect on a strategy you used or a strategy you think you could have used, provide your supervisor with background information/context of something that is happening, or ask a question of your supervisor. Finally, use your self-reflection to develop two targeted goals for your next GoReact lesson. How will you work to develop these skills and monitor your performance?

APPENDIX B: CLASSROOM ANALYSIS: LESSON DELIVERY

Sample Assignment

Directions: Make arrangements with your mentor teacher to complete this observation. Ideally, this will take place during direct instruction, when students are seated at their desks.

Use one sheet of paper to sketch the classroom. Include desks or tables and the teaching area. Please do the following during the observation:

- *One student responds*: record a tally on the desk of a student to indicate an individual response.
- *Total number of individual responses*: _____.
- *All students respond*: Tally in table under correct category.

Oral Response (Choral)	Oral Response (Partner)	Written Response	Action Response

- *Monitoring*: record an "M" on a student's desk if the teacher stops and looks at the student's work or in any other way interacts with the student.
- *Feedback*: Tally instances of elaborated feedback.

Contingent, Specific Feedback on Performance	Total

Using the data above, respond to the following questions:

1. Were many responses elicited during the lesson?
2. Were all students given opportunities to respond?
3. Were individual responses distributed across students?
4. Did the teacher move around the room and monitor?
5. During monitoring, did the teacher connect with many students?
6. Did the teacher affirm, honor, and praise students?
7. Any additional observations?

APPENDIX C: CLASSROOM PRACTICES VIDEO SELF-ANALYSIS GUIDED REFLECTION TOOL

Name: _____ Date: _____

Evidence-Based Practices: The "Big Five"[1]

1. Maximize structure in your classroom.
2. Post, teach, review, monitor, and reinforce positively stated expectations.
3. Actively engage students in observable ways.
4. Establish a continuum of strategies for responding to appropriate behavior.
5. Establish a continuum of strategies for responding to inappropriate behavior.

☐ I read/discussed "The Big Five" and Reviewed Operational Definitions of Teaching Strategies

Directions: Watch 15 minutes of your teaching video. Select video clips where you are actively engaged with students for the best results (i.e., direct instruction). As you watch the video, put a tally when you observe the following:

Teaching Strategies	Tally		Total
Prompts			
Feedback (instructional, behavioral)	POSITIVE, SPECIFIC	CORRECTIVE	
Varied Opportunities to respond	1 STUDENT	MORE THAN 1 ONGOING	
Relational Contact			

In a few sentences for each question, discuss and respond in writing to the following reflection questions after watching the video clip:

1. How do you maximize structure?
2. Have students been taught routines and expectations in class? Is there a need for any reteaching?
3. Were any prompts used? If so, what was the result? How can you use them in the future?
4. How was specific, contingent praise used during this video? What was the purpose and possible result? Can you identify a time that it *could have been* used?
5. Were OTRs appropriately engaging for the type of instruction? Was there some variation to the types of OTRs used (e.g., more than one student, gestural)? Were students actively or passively engaged?

6. How did you scaffold this lesson with verbal prompts, visual prompts, and questioning?
7. On a scale of 1–10 (1 being lowest, 10 being highest), rate the level of active supervision (walking/looking around, closely monitoring students) by adults. What was the result?
8. Did you notice any instances of relational contact? How is this useful? Are there ways to increase these positive teacher-student interactions?
9. What would you like to change/improve this week regarding your use of these skills?

Operational Definitions of Teaching Behaviors[2]

SPECIFIC PRAISE: Any instance of verbal statement and/or gesture made by the teacher directed at an individual student or a group of students that indicates the <u>teacher's contingent approval of desired student behavior while explicitly identifying the behavior for which the</u> praise <u>is given.</u>

> Examples: Specific positive feedback that refers to a student's behavior, such as "Beautiful job reading that excerpt to the class"; positive comments on productivity relative to the task, such as "I appreciate how everyone is working so hard on this assignment"; adding points, tokens, or stickers for any individual or class-wide activity while specifying how those were earned; thanking students for specific behaviors, such as "Thank you for being kind to your classmate."
>
> Non-examples: General directions or instructions; general approval statements; approval gestures; adding points, tokens, or stickers for any individual or class-wide activities without specifying how those were earned; thanking students without specifying for what; encouraging statements without specifying behavior.

OPPORTUNITIES TO RESPOND: A teacher behavior that invites or solicits a student response. Responses from students can be verbal, written, or gestural.

> **Examples**: A teacher asks their students a question and calls on one student to answer (1 student); a teacher asks students to turn to a partner to discuss a topic (more than 1 student); a teacher asks students to give a thumbs up or down if they agree/disagree with a statement (more than 1 student).
> **Non-examples**: A teacher asks a question and then answers it.

PROMPTS/PRE-CORRECT: A verbal or non-verbal <u>teacher-delivered cue</u> that provides students with information about the behavior desired in a given circumstance, <u>delivered before the behavior is expected</u>.

> **Examples**: Prior to asking a question, a teacher may remind students to raise their hands if they want to respond; a teacher may remind students how to get their attention during independent work time prior to the start of independent work time; a teacher may use a hand signal to indicate that they would like students to clear their workspace prior to the start of class; a teacher may remind students of specific expected behaviors on the playground prior to going to recess.
> **Non-examples**: Reminding students of expected behavior after they have made a behavioral error; providing reminders that are general. (e.g., "Remember to be good on the playground!")

RELATIONAL CONTACTS: Any instance in which the teacher provides <u>positive verbal non-contingent attention</u> to a student or group of students.

> **Examples**: Greeting students individually; asking questions about students' personal lives; following up with a

student (for example, asking, "Kate, is this clearer now that we've practiced the sequence all together?"); sharing personal experience to enhance academic material or provide context for social-emotional learning or behavioral management; using humor.

Non-examples: Offering general student praise; making jokes at students' expense; gossiping; addressing individual students without using their names (for example, commenting, "Hey, the girl in a purple shirt" or "You two at the table in the back"); making jokes or comments inappropriate to the school setting; using sarcasm (for example, saying, "Thanks for finally joining us" in sarcastic tone); making harsh or critical comments.

Notes

1. Simonsen, B., Fairbanks, S., Briesch, A., Myers, D., & Sugai, G. (2008). Evidence-based practices in classroom management: Considerations for research to practice. *Education and Treatment of Children, 31*(3), 351–380.
2. Adapted from BESTed Observation, University of Massachusetts.

7

Collaboration in and Beyond the Classroom

Throughout her coursework, Kennedy heard a lot about the importance of educators' collaborating with their colleagues, students' families, and professional networks. As a student teacher, she observed her cooperating teacher participate in team meetings and professional learning communities with her colleagues, engage her students' families in their children's educations, and be an active member of her state's literacy association. Kennedy could see how much her cooperating teacher benefited from each of these collaborations, and she aspired to do the same as she stepped into her role as a new educator. So, throughout her student teaching experience, she joined her cooperating teacher in meetings as often as possible, participated in student conferences, and was even able to attend a professional conference. These collaborative experiences provided her with the foundation she needed to confidently begin her career as an educator.

Collaboration Is Necessary for Positive Outcomes

No one can effectively educate students of varying backgrounds and support needs about a wide range of topics in a complex and ever-changing world alone. Educators need to rely on colleagues, families, and professional organizations to "share the load" throughout their careers, support one another when challenges arise, celebrate achievements, and continue their lifelong learning. Collaboration is identified as a key high-leverage domain for teachers working with students with disabilities (Aceves & Kennedy, 2024). It has been shown to bolster both student and teacher outcomes (Vangrieken et al., 2015).

Shand and Goddard (2024) discovered that, over time, teachers learn to collaborate more effectively AND that teachers who collaborate effectively tend to use differentiated instruction more frequently. This collaboration also leads to a stronger focus on student learning, increased collective responsibility, and heightened trust among teachers, as well as among teachers, students, and parents. Furthermore, improvements in instructional quality, the learning environment, and social relationships accelerate as well. Each of these elements is known to enhance student achievement and teacher efficacy. Moreover, when teachers engage in high-quality collaboration, it is likely to lead to improvements in student achievement in math and reading (Ronfeldt et al., 2015). Table 7.1 provides further research on the significance of teacher collaboration.

Collaboration among professionals is most effective when all members share a common understanding of best practices. This

TABLE 7.1 Research on Teacher Collaboration

	What Does the Research Say?
Research Study	*Key Takeaway*
Hargreaves, 2019	This article examines 30 years of research on teacher collaboration and outlines important considerations for the most beneficial design for teacher collaboration. Effective designs include professional learning communities, collaborative planning, school networks, data teams, and peer review.
Hoppey & Mickelson, 2017	This qualitative research study examines the structures that contribute to preservice teachers' developing collaboration skills and to their ability to support students with disabilities in inclusive classrooms. Results suggest that collaboration improved preservice teacher instruction for students with disabilities in general education classrooms.

includes building strong relationships, exchanging ideas, actively listening, engaging in open dialogue, and fostering trust. It is also essential to keep in mind that the primary goal of collaboration should be to benefit the students. In this chapter, we explore how teaching in an inclusive classroom requires effective collaboration with colleagues, families, and professional organizations. We also share insights and ideas for effectively using your voice to advocate for policies that support teachers, students, and communities.

Collaboration with Colleagues

Teams and Professional Learning Communities

In today's educational environment, most schools encourage and often expect educators to participate on instructional teams. These teams engage in a variety of activities, including taking part in professional development opportunities, monitoring student achievement, problem-solving, planning lessons and instruction, and taking care of any other logistical details associated with student needs. Some schools organize teams by grade level or subject department, while others adopt vertical teaming structures that include representatives from each grade level or department. Additionally, some schools utilize interdisciplinary teams that combine multiple subject areas.

For many educators, especially those who are new to the profession, support teams play a vital role in their success. These teams offer support with both long-term goals and the everyday tasks and challenges that come with being an effective educator. Research shows that educators with a strong connection to a professional community experience lower levels of burnout, which contributes to a greater sense of well-being at work (Sullanmaa et al., 2024). Additionally, educators are more motivated to participate in professional learning involving collaboration (Durksen et al., 2017).

When collaboration is a more formalized process, educators may be a part of a professional learning community (PLC). The definition of a PLC can vary among educational settings. Hudson

(2024) offers the following definition based on a recent literature review:

> A professional learning community is a group of educators motivated by continuous improvement, collective responsibility, and mutual goal alignment, who engage collaboratively in professional learning to increase educator effectiveness and to improve student outcomes. This is achieved by the educators sharing and critically interrogating their practice in an ongoing, reflective, inclusive, learning-oriented, and growth-promoting way, underpinned by a high level of collegial trust and a supportive school environment.
>
> (p. 652)

Many schools utilize a PLC model to review student outcome data, make decisions about programming and support structures, reflect on instructional practices, and bolster teacher learning. Throughout your student teaching experience, join team and PLC meetings alongside your cooperating teacher to see how this form of collaboration can positively impact both student and educator outcomes.

Special Educators

As a general education teacher with an inclusive classroom, you will undoubtedly, and fortunately, be working alongside at least one special educator. Collaborating with special educators provides you not only with much-needed expertise for supporting students with disabilities but also with a partner in your students' educations. While a special educator may develop a particular student's IEP and deliver specialized instruction, you are ultimately responsible for that student's success in your classroom. Coordination and consistency between you and the special educator increase the likelihood that your student will meet IEP goals, benefit from instruction, and experience a positive learning environment.

There are different models of collaboration between general educators and special educators. Each model meets different needs and contexts. While schools may choose how they approach special education support based on their student needs, available resources, and other contextual factors, decisions must nonetheless aim to meet each student's needs as identified within their IEP. Students with IEPs may receive services in a resource room or within your classroom. Both approaches require you to collaborate with the special educator about scheduling, instructional planning, progress monitoring, data collection, communication with the family, and alignment with additional service providers. You can foster a collaborative approach by sharing responsibility and accountability and by being approachable, open-minded, and flexible. It may be disruptive to have a student pulled out of your room during a key instructional block or to have a small group meet in the back of your room. Try to be accommodating. Remember that special educators are trying to match the logistical and instructional needs of numerous educators, paraprofessionals, support providers, and students. Most people look at a special educator's planner and are amazed by the many puzzle pieces they are trying to fit into any single day.

One way to minimize some of the scheduling and logistical challenges associated with the delivery of special education is to use the co-teaching model. In this model, a general educator and a special educator work collaboratively to provide effective instruction to a single group of students. These pairs of educators may swap turns teaching content while the other observes or assists students; they may each teach half the class at the same time; they may choose to have one educator lead instruction for the whole group while the other supports a small group; or they may each lead a station as students rotate between educators and independent learning (Barron & Friend, 2024). Co-teaching requires common planning time, an appreciation of each other's professional role and expertise, and administrative support. When co-teaching is implemented effectively, students are able to remain within the classroom throughout most of the day, leading to increased consistency, fewer transitions, and more instructional time. This may explain why students with disabilities often demonstrate improved academic achievement when compared to those in self-contained classrooms (King-Sears et al., 2021).

Paraprofessionals

Paraprofessionals, also known as teaching assistants or educational technicians, play a vital role in schools. They work alongside certified teachers to deliver instruction and provide support in various settings within the learning community. Each state has different regulations regarding the qualifications and responsibilities of paraprofessionals. As you begin your student teaching, look for opportunities to learn more about their roles in your classroom and school.

Many paraprofessionals work with students who have disabilities, providing the additional support necessary for these students to be successfully integrated into general education classrooms. As the general education teacher, you may be responsible for orienting and guiding paraprofessionals as well as for preparing lesson plans for them. Developing respect for one another is crucial to your successful collaboration. Indeed, remember that paraprofessionals may have worked with specific students for several years; this means they often have in-depth knowledge of effective strategies for working with a particular student as well as of their triggers for escalated behavior, and they can often offer important insights. It's essential to honor and value this background knowledge to provide effective support. Make sure to find time to meet with any paraprofessionals working in your classroom to collaboratively clarify roles, responsibilities, and expectations at the onset of your work together (Yates et al., 2020). This will help everyone feel more confident, and it sets the stage for a positive working relationship.

Paraprofessionals who do not work with specific students have a variety of roles. Some assist in special education resource rooms, while others deliver interventions to students identified as needing advanced support with academics or behavior. Additionally, paraprofessionals may supervise students during lunch, recess, transitions between classes, study halls, or other, less structured times of the day. Regardless of their specific roles, when paraprofessionals receive adequate training, student outcomes can improve (Clotfelter et al., 2016), including for those students with disabilities (Brock & Carter, 2013; Walker et al., 2020). Collaborating effectively with paraprofessionals can significantly enhance your instructional impact, especially for students who require additional support. If you have the opportunity to work with paraprofessionals, remember to recognize their important contributions to the educational environment.

Families

If you recently took a course focused on Educational Psychology, it is likely that you learned about psychologist Urie Bronfenbrenner's socio-ecological systems theory of human development (Bronfenbrenner, 1975). This "systems within systems" theory examines how environments interact over time to meet the needs of children to positively affect their learning and development (Bronfenbrenner, 2005). Research has shown that when we apply Bronfenbrenner's theory to educational settings by engaging families as partners in their children's educations, we see positive outcomes for their academic performance (Stanley & Kuo, 2022). Table 7.2 provides suggestions for ways to build positive, collaborative relationships with families during student teaching. With so much to accomplish during this time, working to develop your family collaboration skills sometimes takes a back seat to being prepared for all of your other day-to-day responsibilities. That said, finding time to focus on developing these skills now will contribute to building your confidence as a new teacher. We promise that this is time well spent, for both you and your students.

A final consideration for developing your family collaboration skills and self-efficacy is to be mindful of factors that are and are not within your control. It is easy for educators to attribute difficulties with students as issues stemming from the home environment, or to a parent's lack of responsiveness or to a lack of concern for their child's education. We have to be careful not to make assumptions when caregivers appear to be disinterested or when they lack follow-through on supporting their child at home. Playing the "blame game" when it comes to frustrations with parents and caregivers can leave us feeling powerless. Continue to build bridges, even when you do not feel your efforts are being reciprocated, and work to be patient

TABLE 7.2 Key Strategies for Successful Collaboration with Families

Key Strategy	Considerations for Application
Establish Trust and Open Communication	• Introduce yourself early on in your placement by sharing a welcome letter and positive phone call home. • Ask your cooperating teacher if you can contribute to classroom communication methods, such as newsletters, emails, and apps such as Remind and ClassDojo. • Communicate regularly to share successes and to provide class updates.
Approach Families as Partners and Be Culturally Responsive	• View parents and caregivers as experts of their children. Ask to hear their experiences, insights, and concerns. • Avoid using educational jargon in meetings with caregivers. • Learn about your students' cultural backgrounds, languages, and family structure. When needed, use a translator.
Use Effective Communication Skills to Identify Shared Goals	• Use active and reflective listening when communicating with parents so they feel heard and valued. • Use strengths-based rather than deficit-based language when talking to families about their children. Highlight capabilities and frame concerns as challenges and opportunities for growth.
Build and Maintain Positive Relationships	• Attend events outside of the school day to learn about the community and make yourself visible to families. • Create resources for families to share information about community supports and ways for caregivers to support student learning at home.
Working with Families of Struggling Learners and Students with Disabilities	• Help to prepare for, attend, and participate in student IEP meetings and family conferences. • Be proactive and responsive. Be sure to acknowledge concerns and involve families in problem-solving. • Provide examples of how an IEP or 504 plan will be implemented in your classroom. • Be respectful of family perspectives. • Share celebrations of successes with parents and caregivers.

and have empathy, especially when it feels hard to do so. Maintaining a positive attitude when collaborating with families is empowering; it will help you to avoid burnout and not lose sight of your many successes.

Key Takeaways

♦ *Collaboration among professionals and families is most effective when all members share a common understanding of best practices. This includes building strong relationships, exchanging ideas, actively listening, engaging in open dialogue, and fostering trust.*
♦ *Strong communication skills go a long way toward effective collaboration. Active listening, shared problem-solving, and non-judgmental interactions are essential components of this process. Avoid personalizing others' behavior, and maintain a professional, positive attitude.*

Stepping into the Field of Education

Professional Organizations

The student teaching semester is a great time to learn about and become involved with professional organizations and networks beyond your school and teacher preparation program, which will enhance your developing teaching practice as well as your long-term career. Many professional organizations have national, statewide, and regional networks, and they offer support to student teachers through webinars, workshops, conferences, and practice briefs. Seeking out volunteer and leadership opportunities can provide invaluable experience and can help you build your resume. Your involvement can also provide you with networking opportunities and job search support. We expand upon this in the next chapter. As a student, you are likely able to join most professional organizations as a student member, which offers a substantial discount. While not exhaustive, Table 7.3 provides a list of several professional organizations that may be of interest to you.

Policy and Advocacy

To a student teacher, the world of education policy may feel complicated and filled with conflict, and perhaps you would much rather focus on your students, lesson plans, and your growing practice. That's fair; we understand! That said, whatever your interest level is when it comes to being politically engaged, *politics*

TABLE 7.3 Professional Organizations in Education

Area	Organization Name
Special Education	Council for Exceptional Children (CEC)
Behavior	Association for Positive Behavior Support (APBS)
English Language Arts	National Council of Teachers of English (NCTE)
Mathematics	National Council of Teachers of Mathematics (NCTM)
Science	National Science Teaching Organization (NSTO)
Literacy	International Literacy Association (ILA)
Dyslexia	International Dyslexia Association (IDA)
Bilingual Education	The National Association for Bilingual Education (NABE)

is interested in you, the teaching profession, your students, and what happens in your classroom. You are about to step into a world that is affected in substantial and numerous ways by policymakers and legislation housed at the local, state, and federal levels. This impacts the resources that you have and the work that you do on a daily basis, and it will continue to do so throughout your career in education. So, we encourage you to become politically informed and to begin to think about what advocacy might look like for the teaching profession, for you, and for your students—especially students with disabilities and those who are from marginalized backgrounds whose voices have been disenfranchised. After all, educators are on the front lines of this field, and we have first-hand knowledge of current challenges and day-to-day needs. No policymaker knows your community and classroom better than YOU! In case you need more reasons to jump in, Table 7.4 provides research demonstrating positive effects of teacher advocacy.

In her book *Advocating for the Common Good,* Jane West (2024) presents a framework called "the four Ps" (people, politics, process, and policy) that can help educators understand and conceptualize policy-making in the field of special education. As a student teacher, developing your understanding of the four Ps can help you to effectively advocate for policies that positively affect teachers and students, including your students with disabilities. First, it is important to understand the *people* involved in making education policy, including the executive branch, congress, interest groups, experts, and even social media platforms.

TABLE 7.4 Research on Teacher Advocacy

	What Does the Research Say?
Research Study	Key Takeaway
Raymond et al., 2024	This study surveyed teachers to learn about their perspectives on advocacy skills, strengths, and challenges. Results suggest that when teachers can overcome a variety of barriers, they feel empowered to advocate for critical issues.
Hatch et al., 2005	Through a case study investigation, this research study highlights how teachers—regardless of leadership position—can successfully influence policy and advocate for positive school and classroom reform.

Learning how various people communicate can help us to be more effective advocates. *Politics* also impacts policymaking, for example, and learning about your representatives' political party affiliations and whether or not a party is in the majority is important for advocacy, as is exercising your right to vote. Finally, understanding the *process* for policymaking can help us to be strategic advocates for good *policy*. Below we share several ideas for how student teachers can begin to take action for their students, for their careers, and for the larger field of American education.

A Getting Started Checklist for Student Teacher Advocacy

- Become and stay informed by following local, state, and federal education policy issues. See the national and state branch National Education Association (NEA), American Federation of Teachers (AFT), and the Council for Exceptional Children (CEC) websites to read about their positions on current issues.
- Consider becoming a member of these organizations and participating in advocacy efforts. This can be as simple as sending an email to a representative.
- Attend a school board meeting to learn about local issues, concerns, and priorities. Consider sharing your perspective and experiences with school board members.
- Become an advocate at the school level by voicing concerns regarding student needs.

Key Takeaways

- Recognize that your efforts to become politically engaged at the local, state, and national levels can have positive outcomes for teachers and students.
- The four Ps provide a framework to help you start implementing effective advocacy skills.

Perspectives in Practice: Professionalism Beyond the Classroom

Supporting Your Student Teachers Beyond Your Classroom

Alex has been a cooperating teacher for many student teachers over the years. Each time Alex has a new student teacher, he encourages them to be an active participant in planning for department-level meetings, committee work, and PLC activities. Sometimes, this means the student teacher analyzes grade-level student data to determine potential shifts in student groupings. Other times, the student teacher gets to connect with teachers across the district to see how curriculum decisions are made. And still, in other cases, the student teacher is able to learn from other PLC members about how they are implementing a new program in their classroom. Alex says that the student teachers he has mentored have found these experiences to be invaluable because they provide insight into the breadth and depth of the teaching profession. Many of his student teachers were unaware of the many roles and expectations required of teachers beyond delivering instruction in the classroom until they participated in these experiences.

Recognizing Problems and Using Your Voice

Three weeks into his student teaching semester, James got an early morning text from his cooperating teacher sharing that she had come down with an illness and would be out for the day. When James arrived at school, the school secretary informed him that there were no available substitutes that day. As a result, the students in James's second-grade inclusive class would be split up among the other second-grade classrooms. The secretary suggested that James split his time between rooms that day. James was immediately concerned, especially for Chloe, his student with autism who thrived on structure and routine, and Luca, his student who had just started a behavior support plan. While everyone made it through the day, James realized just how challenging this was for both the teachers and students.

The next day, James's cooperating teacher shared that there is a widespread teacher shortage and substitute teacher shortage across the state. Their district paid a slightly lower daily substitute rate than did other local districts, leaving them without substitutes on a regular basis. James's cooperating teacher felt this had a detrimental effect on student learning, and it was draining for teachers, leaving some to feel burned out.

James shared this experience with his student teaching cohort at their weekly seminar meeting. His seminar instructor introduced the class to their statewide chapter of the National Educators Association website, which had a section dedicated to current policy issues in education—one of them was the teacher shortage. James decided to use what he learned on the website to advocate for better policies to address the teacher and substitute teacher shortage. He sent an email to local school board members and his state representatives. James was happy to have found a way to use his voice to advocate for his students. Sharing his story with those who make decisions about education practices felt empowering.

Mentorship Corner: Supporting Effective Collaboration

Tips for Cooperating Teachers

- ♦ Student teachers may feel uncomfortable asking to attend staff meetings, professional development events, and PLC meetings. Invite and encourage them to come along! Explain the purpose and benefits of these collaborations.
- ♦ If a paraprofessional is a part of your classroom community, provide opportunities for your student teacher to participate in any planning and coordination that occurs.

- Support your student teacher with developing family communication (e.g., newsletters, emails).
- Let your student teacher be a part of the conference preparation process. Then, allow them to attend conferences and, when possible, lead a conference or two.
- Tell your student teacher about any professional memberships you hold and explain the benefits of doing so. If the organization holds events, consider asking your student teacher to join you.

Tips for University Supervisors
- Ask your student teachers how they collaborate with school staff outside of their classrooms. Make attendance at staff meetings, PLCs, and co-teaching planning meetings a required component of the student teaching experience.
- Facilitate connections between student teachers and local professional organizations. If applicable, encourage them to join the student chapter of their state's educator association.

Practice and Reflect: Application Activities to Support Your Development

In Your Classroom

- Ask your cooperating teacher about how they collaborate with others and join in on any opportunities you can!
- Work with your cooperating teacher to share responsibility for family communication and conference preparation and attend IEP and other student support meetings.

In Seminar or Post-observation Meetings

- Attend family conferences while at school and share your experiences with your cohort. Brainstorm solutions to any challenging interactions you observe. Be sure to maintain student and family confidentiality.
- Choose a policy issue that is important to you and the peers in your cohort. Write letters to local, state, and national representatives to voice opinions and share experiences with those in power.
- Make plans with your cohort to attend a school board meeting to observe the policy-making process at the local level.

On Your Own

- Research professional organizations within your state and region. Join and attend events that interest you.
- Join the student chapter of your state's teacher association, if available.

Teacher Toolbox: Resources for Further Exploration

- ◆ The Council for Exceptional Children and the CEEDAR Center offer guidance through High Leverage Practices: Practice Area One - Collaboration.[1]
- ◆ HLP 1: Collaborate with professionals to increase student success.
- ◆ HLP 3: Collaborate with families to support student learning and secure needed services.
- ◆ This article, "How Educators Can Use PLCs for Innovation and Support,[2]" shares tips for successful PLCs and provides links to organizations offering PLCs in specific topic areas.
- ◆ Try the 5-15-45 Tool[3] from the TIES Center to use your collaboration time effectively.
- ◆ Building and Sustaining a Collaborative Educational Team: Teachers and Paraprofessionals[4] examines common challenges between teachers and paraeducators and provides helpful strategies for strengthening collaboration.
- ◆ Encourage families to promote positive behavior at home by sharing this guide, Supporting Families with PBIS at Home.[5]
- ◆ This Classroom Family Engagement Rubric[6] provides actionable steps to promote family engagement.
- ◆ The following practice guides can support families of students with disabilities as they prepare for IEP meetings:
    - ◆ Helping Families Prepare for an IEP Meeting[7]
    - ◆ Strengthening Family Participation in Addressing Behavior in an IEP.[8]
- ◆ The National Education Association's Advocating for Change page[9] keeps you updated on current education

issues while suggesting ways to take action. You can join the organization[10] for additional benefits.
- The Council for Exceptional Children is involved in policy and advocacy[11] for students with disabilities and their educators. This page offers many resources including advocacy events and networks.

Notes

1. https://highleveragepractices.org/collaboration
2. https://www.edutopia.org/article/how-educators-can-use-plcs-for-innovation-and-support/
3. https://tiescenter.org/topics/inclusive-instruction/5-15-45-tool
4. https://journals.sagepub.com/doi/10.1177/00400599241231215
5. https://www.pbis.org/resource/supporting-families-with-pbis-at-home
6. https://www.pbis.org/resource/classroom-family-engagement-rubric
7. https://www.pbis.org/resource/helping-families-prepare-for-an-iep-meeting
8. https://www.pbis.org/resource/strengthening-family-participation-in-addressing-behavior-in-an-iep
9. https://www.nea.org/advocating-for-change
10. https://www.nea.org/
11. https://exceptionalchildren.org/policy-and-advocacy

References

Aceves, T. C., & Kennedy, M. J. (Eds.). (2024). *High-leverage practices for students with disabilities.* Council for Exceptional Children.

Barron, T., & Friend, M. (2024). Co-teaching: Are we there yet? *Journal of Educational and Psychological Consultation,* 1–26. https://doi.org/10.1080/10474412.2024.2422895

Brock, M. E., & Carter, E. W. (2013). A systematic review of paraprofessional-delivered educational practices to improve outcomes for students with intellectual and developmental disabilities. *Research and*

Practice for Persons with Severe Disabilities, 38(4), 211–221. https://doi.org/10.1177/154079691303800401

Bronfenbrenner, U. (1975). Reality and research in the ecology of human development. *Proceedings of the American Philosophical Society, 119*(6), 439–469. http://www.jstor.org/stable/986378

Bronfenbrenner, U. (2005). *Making human beings human: Bioecological perspectives on human development.* Sage.

Clotfelter, C. T., Hemelt, S. W., & Ladd, H. F. (2016). *Teaching assistants and nonteaching staff: Do they improve student outcomes?* Working Paper 169. *National Center for Analysis of Longitudinal Data in Education Research (CALDER.*

Durksen, T. L., Klassen, R. M., & Daniels, L. M. (2017). Motivation and collaboration: The keys to a developmental framework for teachers' professional learning. *Teaching and Teacher Education, 67,* 53–66. https://doi.org/10.1016/j.tate.2017.05.011

Hargreaves, A. (2019). Teacher collaboration: 30 years of research on its nature, forms, limitations and effects. *Teachers and Teaching, 25*(5), 603–621. https://doi.org/10.1080/13540602.2019.1639499

Hatch, T., White, M. E., & Faigenbaum, D. (2005). Expertise, credibility, and influence: How teachers can influence policy, advance research, and improve performance. *Teachers College Record, 107*(5), 1004–1035. https://doi.org/10.1111/j.1467-9620.2005.00502.x

Hoppey, D., & Mickelson, A. M. (2017). Partnership and coteaching: Preparing preservice teachers to improve outcomes for students with disabilities. *Action in Teacher Education, 39*(2), 187–202. https://doi.org/10.1080/01626620.2016.1273149

Hudson, C. (2024). A conceptual framework for understanding effective professional learning community (PLC) operation in schools. *Journal of Education, 204*(3), 649–659. https://doi.org/10.1177/00220574231197364

King-Sears, M. E., Stefanidis, A., Berkeley, S., & Strogilos, V. (2021). Does co-teaching improve academic achievement for students with disabilities? A meta-analysis. *Educational Research Review, 34,* 100405.

Raymond, K. M., Ethridge, E. A., & Fields, K. (2024). What it takes to be an advocate: Teachers' perceptions of their strengths and challenges. *Action in Teacher Education, 47*(1), 46–62. https://doi.org/10.1080/01626620.2024.2383744

Ronfeldt, M., Farmer, S. O., McQueen, K., & Grissom, J. A. (2015). Teacher collaboration in instructional teams and student achievement. *American Educational Research Journal*, *52*(3), 475–514. https://doi.org/10.3102/0002831215585562

Shand, R., & Goddard, R. D. (2024). The relationship between teacher collaboration and instructional practices, instructional climate, and social relations. *Educational Policy*, 0(0). https://doi.org/10.1177/08959048241278290

Stanley, K., & Kuo, N. (2022). "It takes a village": Approaching the development of school-family community partnerships through Bronfenbrenner's socio-ecological perspectives. *Journal of Human Sciences and Extension*, *10*(1), 13. https://doi.org/10.54718/CQBW6379

Sullanmaa, J., Pyhältö, K., Pietarinen, J., & Soini, T. (2024). Teacher agency in the professional community and association with burnout: A longitudinal person-centred approach. *Research Papers in Education*, *39*(4), 539–559. https://doi.org/10.1080/02671522.2023.2178028

Vangrieken, K., Dochy, F., Raes, E., & Kyndt, E. (2015). Teacher collaboration: A systematic review. *Educational Research Review*, *15*, 17–40, https://doi.org/10.1016/j.edurev.2015.04.002

Walker, V. L., Douglas, K. H., Douglas, S. N., & D'Agostino, S. R. (2020). Paraprofessional-implemented systematic instruction for students with disabilities: A systematic literature review. *Education and Training in Autism and Developmental Disabilities*, *55*(3), 303–317. https://www.jstor.org/stable/27077922

West, J. E. (2024). *Advocating for the common good: People, politics, process, and policy on Capitol Hill*. Rowman & Littlefield.

Yates, P. A., Chopra, R. V., Sobeck, E. E., Douglas, S. N., Morano, S., Walker, V. L., & Schulze, R. (2020). Working with paraeducators: Tools and strategies for planning, performance feedback, and evaluation. *Intervention in School and Clinic*, *56*(1), 43–50. https://doi.org/10.1177/1053451220910740

8

Navigating Challenges and Looking Ahead

As the final bell rings, marking the end of Taylor's final day of student teaching, she feels a mix of emotions. Thinking back to the uncertainty and nerves she felt on her first day, Taylor is grateful for this experience. There were some challenges with student behavior, lessons that didn't quite go as planned, and late nights of preparing and catching up with grading. Overall, however, Taylor recognizes how much she has grown as a teacher, and she feels a sense of pride when thinking about the relationships she has built with her students and the school community. While Taylor is motivated to finally become a certified teacher and find her first teaching position, the next steps feel a bit daunting. She wonders where to begin and how to best set herself up for a successful start in her first year of teaching in her very own inclusive classroom.

Taylor's experience reflects the next step in the journey to becoming a teacher. Moving from your teacher preparation program to your first year of teaching in an inclusive classroom is an exciting yet challenging transition. This chapter is here to help guide you through this transition with confidence and a clear sense of direction. First, we want to offer guidance about how to navigate common challenges of student teaching effectively. We'll then talk about the importance of reflection at the end of your student teaching experience and about how to identify the lessons that will shape your teaching career.

Next, we'll consider the certification and job search process. Finding the right classroom for you isn't just about getting a job; ideally, it's about finding the best fit for you. We'll discuss how to prepare for interviews as well as factors to consider once you have an offer, such as compensation and benefits, new teacher induction programs, and the school climate.

The work doesn't end once you land your first job! This chapter will provide practical advice to help you to start strong—from preparing for your first days to building relationships with colleagues and mentors and connecting with your school community. You'll also find tips on managing stress, avoiding burnout, and cultivating a sense of belonging as you settle into your role.

Finally, we'll look beyond your first year at how to continue growing as an educator. Whether pursuing advanced certifications, engaging in professional development, or exploring new teaching strategies, you'll learn how to keep evolving and thriving in your career. Whether you're eager to jump into your first teaching position or feel overwhelmed by what lies ahead, we hope this chapter will support you in this process. Let's get started!

Common Challenges

Classroom Management

It is likely that, prior to beginning student teaching, you completed a required classroom management course; nonetheless, you may still feel somewhat unprepared in this area. This is a very common feeling among student teachers (Flower et al., 2016). Generalizing the theories, research, and practices you learned through coursework and implementing effective classroom management practices is challenging for a wide range of reasons. So, our advice is to first give yourself some grace and recognize that this is difficult. Then, carefully observe your cooperating teacher and arrange to visit other classrooms with the intention of observing specific classroom management practices. Reread chapters in this book focused on the classroom environment, and remember to embed reminders to use specific practices, such as behavior-specific praise, into your lesson plans to help you build effective habits. Finally, ask for feedback and support in this area, especially when you are trying to support students who have behavioral challenges. As you think about moving to your first year, focus on how you will get off to a successful start. Spend time now, while this is fresh in your mind, making plans for your first weeks of school. At the end of this chapter, please see an example assignment, the Classroom Practices Implementation Plan (Appendix A), that can assist you with organizing your ideas.

Embracing Feedback and Filtering Criticism

Every student teacher is different and begins the semester with varied experiences hearing and receiving feedback, both in the classroom and beyond. In addition, cooperating teachers have varied experience coaching student teachers and giving feedback, and some may feel either more or less comfortable in this area (Altan & Sağlamel, 2015). Regardless of experience, we know that feedback is an essential component of student teaching and that high-quality, specific performance feedback will undoubtedly make a positive contribution to your development (Won et al., 2019). Here are some ideas for how to receive and embrace feedback:

- ♦ Ask for specific feedback in competency areas prior to teaching a lesson. For example, "Can you watch for how I manage to get and sustain the students' attention during whole group math instruction? My mind is often so focused on the content, I am unsure about how well students are attending and remaining on-task." Or, "I am struggling with pacing during small group reading intervention. Can you observe me this afternoon and provide feedback on the pace of instruction?"
- ♦ When you receive feedback that is general and/or confusing, ask for clarification. For example, if your university supervisor shares that you need to work on student engagement, ask for a few specific ideas about how you

can improve in this area. Jot down these ideas and embed them into your lesson plans so that you can practice them. When your supervisor visits for your next observation, let them know that you have worked on using these strategies and ask for further feedback.
- Develop emotional resilience and a growth mindset for when you receive feedback, especially if it feels harsh or critical. Practice your emotional response outside of school. How will you feel when you receive feedback? How can you acknowledge your feelings and remind yourself that discomfort or uncertainty is temporary? Prior to responding, ensure that you have considered the feedback and filtered out unhelpful criticism, and then ask for clarification if needed.
- Express gratitude for helpful and specific feedback, and practice self-compassion. Remind yourself that "mistakes" that may feel like our biggest failures are often opportunities for the most growth through self-reflection.

Managing Relationships

Ideally, you have been proactive when it comes to building positive professional relationships during student teaching; still, even with careful attention, relationship challenges can arise throughout the semester. When this happens, it is important to get support from a trusted mentor who can help you to establish a plan to address any issues. Oftentimes, problems occur when expectations are not clear, and communication breaks down. Start by identifying the problems and reflecting on the situation. Take responsibility for any contribution you may have made to worsen the problem by thinking about how you can adjust your own behavior. Remain professional, try to avoid making assumptions about what the other person is thinking or feeling, and do not personalize others' behavior. Once you are in the right frame of mind, initiate communication by asking for time to discuss challenges. When the time comes for a conversation, use "I" statements (e.g., "I feel concerned that I am mishandling student behavior; can we discuss it?") and active listening (e.g., "So it sounds like you have concerns with my classroom management style. I am open to hearing more about how I can improve."). Keep in mind that during student teaching, you are a guest in a classroom, so be willing to be flexible when it comes to adapting your teaching style or approach, even if it is different from what you envision yourself using in the future. Finally, when a relationship is strained, find small ways to show gratitude. This can go a long way.

Stress and Burnout Management

Experiencing stress in the workplace is common for many adults, and sometimes stress can actually be beneficial and protective. Stress is a physical or mental response to a perceived threat or challenge, and a stress reaction to a challenging situation is common, normal, and sometimes even helpful. A manageable amount of short-term stress can help us to be productive and energized, and it can even help us to respond appropriately to potentially dangerous situations (i.e., "fight or flight") (Suzuki, 2021). You will undoubtedly feel stress at times throughout your student teaching semester, and this can be a response to a wide variety of teaching tasks and activities. Both novice and experienced teachers report feeling stressed due to their workload, student behavior and classroom management issues, a lack of autonomy and support, conflicts with colleagues and parents, and more (Agyapong et al., 2022). Moreover, student teachers may feel additional pressure due to frequent observations, evaluations, coursework, and financial demands (Oliver, 2024). As a novice teacher, then, and even throughout your teaching career, it is likely you will experience a number of these stressors.

While it is impossible to prevent all work-related stress during student teaching, it is important to consider ways to both reduce and manage stress so that it doesn't become chronic; continued, long-term stress can lead to feelings of burnout and job dissatisfaction. Table 8.1 offers research about how teacher preparation programs can support you as you move through this journey. The following suggestions may help you to manage stress and avoid burnout:

TABLE 8.1 Research on Teacher Preparation Considerations to Reduce Likelihood of Burnout

	What Does the Research Say?
Research Study	Key Takeaway
Stevenson et al. (2020)	Research has highlighted the importance of classroom management instruction in teacher preparation programs. Teacher education programs should include direct instruction in evidence-based classroom management as part of coursework. As part of field experiences, cooperating teachers and university supervisors should provide modeling of these practices along with scaffolded support and specific performance feedback to student teachers.
Zito et al. (2024)	Researchers conducted a needs assessment to determine the impact of emotional demands on preservice teacher stress and well-being. Findings support the inclusion of stress management training within teacher preparation programs.

- Identify and utilize your support systems at home, at your university, and in your placement. Be open and honest about your experiences, feelings, and frustrations, and seek out a listening ear and ask for advice when you are stressed.
- Prioritize tasks, plan ahead, and focus on what is most important in the moment.
- Be productive at your placement by making use of planning time.
- Set boundaries and schedule breaks at your placement and at home. Maintain hobbies and activities with friends and family during your free time.
- Learn some breathing techniques to help manage the momentary stress that may occur when dealing with a challenging situation at your placement.
- Be reasonable about your expectations of yourself and avoid perfectionism. Embrace mistakes and lessons that do not go as planned; view them as opportunities to grow.
- Be mindful of faculty lunchroom talk. Emotions are contagious. While venting about challenges can feel helpful at times, pay attention to how you are feeling when you

are surrounded by "constant complainers." You could inadvertently take on others' stress as a result.
- Consider your physical health. Go to bed early and stick to a sleep routine. Exercise regularly and eat well. Spend time outdoors. Go for a walk or a hike to clear your mind, even if it is for just 10–15 minutes daily.
- Seek support from a professional if stress begins to feel unmanageable. Colleges and universities often offer mental health support at an on-campus Counseling Center.
- If stress is beginning to feel unmanageable, it is OK to take a mental health day. Discuss this with your cooperating teacher and student teaching supervisor.

While this list of suggestions is not exhaustive, we hope that it helps to provide you with some stress-management ideas. With that said, we do believe that managing teacher stress should not be the sole responsibility of teachers. An afternoon yoga session can be helpful, but if a school environment is toxic and climate conditions are poor, an hour of yoga can only do so much to help. Certain workplace behaviors should not be tolerated, such as discrimination, shaming, bullying, harassment, intimidation, and little to no support for teachers dealing with aggressive or intimidating student behaviors. If you are experiencing any of these things, please speak out and seek the support of your university supervisor.

Key Takeaways

- *Student teachers often experience challenges with classroom management, managing work relationships, and receiving feedback. It is important to avoid personalizing hardships and criticism. Develop emotional resilience when hearing feedback, and ask for clarity, support, and guidance when needed.*
- *Student teachers often experience stress. Practice healthy habits, rely on your support system, set realistic expectations for yourself, and prioritize what is most important. Understand that stress is common and normal, but unhealthy, toxic workplace environments can lead to burnout. Seek help if and when necessary.*

That's a Wrap!

Final Reflection
Chances are that you have spent a great deal of time reflecting on your growing teaching practice throughout the entirety of student teaching. That said, the student teaching semester is typically very hectic, which sometimes leaves little time for deep, intentional reflection across various competency areas. Phasing out of full-time teaching during your final weeks will allow you to spend more time thinking back through the semester about what went well, where you have grown significantly, and how to turn challenging moments into learning experiences. It is common for the university supervisor, cooperating teacher, and the student teacher to have a final meeting. While this is often a meeting for evaluating your performance, ideally this can be a chance to reflect with the help of experienced mentors. In addition to discussing teaching competencies outlined by your teacher preparation program and state department of education, we've provided some additional guided reflection questions in the *Practice and Reflect* section at the end of this chapter.

Building Your Professional Portfolio
Many teacher preparation programs require student teachers to create a professional digital portfolio, and this culminating assignment serves multiple purposes. The process of creating your portfolio fosters self-reflection as you think critically about how specific teaching experiences have contributed to your overall professional development. In addition to highlighting your knowledge and skills, the portfolio documents your progress and demonstrates your abilities across your teacher preparation program and state department of education competencies. It is important to consider your audience when building your portfolio. While your university supervisor may consider the portfolio to be a summative assessment of your experience, potential employers may view the portfolio as part of the interview process.

Tips for Creating Your Professional Portfolio

- Plan ahead. Keep a digital folder to store materials and collect potential portfolio artifacts throughout the semester.
- Obtain photo permission from school and families to include pictures of students but be sure to omit any identifying student information from photos and artifacts, such as student work samples. If you do not have photo permission, blur student faces.
- Choose artifacts that align with teacher preparation competency areas and consider quality over quantity. Include a written description of each artifact, along with a focused reflection sharing what you learned from the artifact and how it demonstrates your proficiency in that competency.
- Find a balance between professionalism and personality. Be sure to proofread your portfolio carefully and to ask for feedback. Highlight your passion for teaching and your commitment to the field of education.

Later in this chapter, we discuss strategies for the job search and tips for successful interviews. We also share additional suggestions for how to best use your digital portfolio as part of this process.

Expressing Your Gratitude and Celebrating Success

Student teachers often feel a variety of emotions as their student teaching placement comes to an end. For some, saying goodbye to the students and mentors to whom they have grown close during this semester can feel like a loss. Still others, like those who have had more challenging experiences, might be counting down the days and feeling a sense of relief to see the end in sight. For most, it is likely a mix of both. All of these feelings are normal and valid. Finding support from your cohort of fellow student teachers can be helpful, but keep in mind that everyone has had a unique experience—there is no "right" way to feel at this time.

Many student teachers want to express appreciation to their cooperating teachers and others at their placement who have supported them along the way. There are many ways to do this. Consider handwritten thank-you notes and small tokens of appreciation, such as a plant or book, for your cooperating teacher and students. Making time for a culminating activity, such as a class party or memory-sharing circle, can provide space for both you and your students to say your goodbyes and gain a sense of closure. Keep in mind that your students may feel a sense of loss, too, so it is important that they are aware of your departure and have an opportunity to say goodbye.

Finding Your First Teaching Position in the Inclusive Classroom

Obtaining Your Teacher Certification

The certification process can feel daunting for teacher candidates, particularly at the early stage. There are many hoops to jump through between now and the time you will walk through the door of your first classroom—just make the decision to jump through one hoop at a time. You can do this! We suggest making a plan early that will leave you with plenty of time to understand the requirements, take the required exams, and submit all necessary materials. The process for certification varies by location, so a good place to begin is by looking at your state's department of education website for information about teacher certification. Begin by finding out what tests are required for your certification and/or endorsement area(s), along with any other requirements (trainings, background checks, etc.). Also pay close attention to application deadlines, testing windows, and costs so that you can create a timeline and budget.

Once you are registered for the appropriate exams, it is time to start preparing. Many tests, such as the Praxis Series (Educational Testing Services), have free online practice exams, and additional test prep resources can be purchased (books, courses, practice tests). Consider creating a study group with other student teachers from your cohort who are also preparing to take the exams and seek support from your university supervisor and the teacher certification officer at your college. When test day arrives, think positively—you are prepared for this! Rely on all that you have learned throughout your teacher preparation coursework and time in the classroom. Use the process of elimination and make educated guesses when you are unsure. Pace yourself by flagging difficult questions and coming back to them at the end to avoid spending too much time on any one question. As you work to complete the test, practice relaxation techniques such as deep breathing, and take "mini-breaks" by closing your eyes for a few seconds to rest your brain. Once you have finished the test, spend time reflecting on your performance. It is possible that you will get preliminary results immediately. Celebrate a passing score! If you did not pass, that is OK. Many teacher candidates do not pass the first time, so think of this as a learning experience. You will be better prepared the second time. Reflect on areas of strength and identify areas that you can focus on for additional preparation.

Certification does not end with the completion of your exams. Most states require you to officially apply for your certification through their department of education website. In addition to submitting your passing test scores, you will need to submit college transcripts. Once everything is submitted, it may take several weeks or longer to get a copy of your teacher certification. Many teacher candidates worry that this will interfere with the job search process. Don't worry! School administrators understand that the process takes time. Communicate in your materials where you are in the process, including anticipated dates for graduation and certification.

Job Search Strategies

Finding your first teaching position requires planning, organization, determination, and patience. Keep in mind that school districts are often filling positions right up until the start of the academic year, and in some cases, they begin the year with vacancies. We understand that you are anxious to know where you will land so that you can start preparing, but the actual job search timeline may not line up with your desired timeline. It is critically important to remember that you are finding a good fit for you—a school where you will be successful and supported during your first years. This takes time, and it is possible that your first offer will not be your best offer. Patience is required once again!

Job Search Q&A

Q: *Where can I find job openings for teaching positions?*
A: There are a variety of ways to learn about open teaching positions. Many state departments of education have job boards on their websites that list all open teaching positions across the state. School districts also post openings on their own websites. If possible, sign up for alerts for new positions. In addition to state and district pages, SchoolSpring.com posts positions in the education field in the United States. Websites are very helpful for searching positions, but do not forget to network! Tell everyone you know that you are looking for a teaching position—you never know who might have a connection to a district that is hiring. Post on LinkedIn and your social media pages and ask family and friends to keep their eyes and ears open for you.

Q. *How should I prepare for an interview?*
A: Before your interview, do some background research on the district and the community. Search the website to learn about the district's mission, policies, and achievements. Consider what makes the district unique and how you think you might be able to contribute. Prepare for your interview by practicing your responses to common questions and have a few specific examples to share from your experience student teaching. You will likely be asked to talk about yourself, your interest in teaching, why you are interested in the specific position, and your own career goals. Expect questions about preparation and planning, classroom management and student behavior, collaboration with colleagues, families, and the community, and supporting students from diverse backgrounds, including students with disabilities. As you consider responses to potential questions in each of these areas, have an example ready to go. If possible, bring a tablet or laptop so you can pull up your digital portfolio and make connections between your examples and your portfolio artifacts. Don't be afraid to share challenges that you have

encountered throughout your preservice program; in fact, this can show that you are capable of self-reflection and growth. For example, you might share that you had a student in your placement who displayed very disruptive behavior and that this was a challenging aspect of your experience. Let the committee know all that you did to support the student, what you learned from this, and how this has contributed to your preparedness as a new teacher. Remember that no administrator expects a first-year teacher to have the skills of a veteran; they want a reflective teacher who brings knowledge, passion, creativity, and a collaborative mindset to the position.

In addition to thinking through your responses to the interview committee's questions, come prepared to ask questions of your own. What do you want to know about the position? Remember, the questions that you ask can demonstrate that you are a capable new teacher, so phrase your questions in a way that highlights your strengths. For example, "During my student teaching placement I had the opportunity to sit in on MTSS team meetings, and I felt this was beneficial to my own development and understanding of student needs. Will there be opportunities for me to participate in leadership teams, once I am settled in?" This question shows that you have experience in a particular area and that you are already thinking about how you can make a school-wide contribution in the future.

Finally, PRACTICE! Ask a friend, family member, or a mentor to act as an interviewer. Provide them with a list of potential questions and share your responses. Bonus points if your mock interviewer has experience in the field of education. Preparation is key to a successful interview. It is very natural to feel nervous, but this practice will give you the confidence that will help you to manage your anxiety and make your best impression when you sit down to talk with a hiring committee for real.

Following the interview, it is possible that you will be asked to return for a final round of interviews, and some districts require job candidates to do brief mock lessons. Spend time preparing a high-quality, engaging lesson. Remember to align your assessments with learning objectives and standards and include accommodations for students with disabilities. If possible, choose a topic or content area where you feel most experienced and knowledgeable. Ask for feedback on your lesson from your cooperating teacher, university supervisor, or a friend in your student teaching cohort. Be sure to gather any needed materials and practice your delivery prior to implementing your mock lesson. Once finished, ask the committee for feedback. Following your interview, spend time reflecting on the process as soon as possible, and take notes so that you can refer to them before the next interview. Think about what went well as well as what could have gone better. Is there anything you can do to help you improve for your next interview? Were you able to regulate your emotions effectively, and if not, what can help you to do so in the future? Make a plan for your next steps.

Q. What factors should I consider when I am offered a position?
A: Congratulations! You've been offered a teaching position. Now what? The majority of states in the U.S. are currently reporting widespread teacher shortages, which are more significant in certain fields (e.g., special education) and geographical areas (e.g., urban, rural) (García & Weiss, 2019; Ingersoll & Tran, 2023). While this is problematic for school districts and the students enrolled in them, it does mean that some new teachers can now be a little choosier when finding a job. Do some research to find out about shortages in your area and keep what you've learned in mind as you make decisions about offers.

Prior to accepting a position, you should consider certain important factors so that you make a decision that is in your best interest. When evaluating the compensation, look beyond just the initial offer. What supports for continuing education does the district offer? What will your salary be in 5 or 10 years? Some districts may offer higher starting salaries, but the increases fall off as teachers move up the salary scale; other districts may start teachers at a slightly lower salary but offer bigger increases with time and education level. In many cases, you can compare districts by searching for bargaining contracts between districts and their teachers' unions. Looking across districts can give you some insight into the offer.

In addition to compensation, consider the support available for new teachers. Does the district have a formal teacher induction program? Will you be assigned a teacher mentor? Does your building offer support through instructional coaching? And, lastly, do the best you can to learn about the school climate. What is the teacher turnover rate in the district? If it is high, why so? The bottom line is that you want to land in a position where you will feel supported in your professional growth and where there is a positive, collegial school climate (see Table 8.2).

Key Takeaways

- *When it comes to finding your first teaching position, it is important to start early. Investigate requirements for teacher certification in your state, create a professional portfolio to highlight your unique accomplishments, and begin to network with friends and family to learn about possible openings in your location of interest.*
- *Prepare and practice for your first interviews by role-playing with other student teachers, friends, and family members. Rehearse responses to potential questions, and identify examples from student teaching and your teacher preparation program that highlight your experience.*
- *Do your research on any school district that offers you a position to ensure that it is a supportive place for you to begin your career.*

TABLE 8.2 Research Identifying Impacts of Positive School Climate on Teachers

	What Does the Research Say?
Research Study	*Key Takeaway*
Meristo and Eisenschmidt (2014)	Novice teachers were surveyed about school climate and sense of self-efficacy. Those who were in more supportive school climates had higher levels of self-efficacy, or beliefs about teaching ability.
Johnson (2021)	This research study analyzed survey data from elementary teachers and found that teachers' perceptions of the school environment and teachers' self-beliefs had a direct effect on their intention to transfer and teacher turnover.

Takeaways for a Successful First Year

You did it! You landed your first teaching position. Take time to celebrate your success as you look forward to this next transition and take your first steps from preservice to early career teacher. Take a well-deserved break. As the school year approaches, begin to consider how to best prepare and organize for the first days of school so that you are proactively planning a good start to your first year.

Many new teachers are anxious to set up their new classroom space, yet it is important to do this without emptying your bank account. Ideally, you have landed a position in a school that will supply you with all the materials necessary to get started. Make use of the materials provided by the school and, for any "extras," consider what is absolutely essential to get started. This is another opportunity to let friends and family know that you are setting up your classroom. Some new teachers create "wish lists" on websites to share on social media to help pay for necessary items. Consider checking out consignment shops and yard sales. A little elbow grease and some creativity can help you to create a space that feels like your own. While it is nice to have a well-decorated classroom that feels like a home away from home, a well-organized classroom is really the key to success. Be sure that materials are organized and visible and that all the spaces in your classroom have a purpose.

Once your classroom is ready to go, it is time to revisit classroom management. Reread Chapter 3 to revisit the routines and expectations you will want to teach during the first weeks of school. If you completed the *Classroom Practices Implementation Plan: Reminders for Starting Your Teaching Career* (Appendix A), now is the perfect time to review the plan and put your reminder checklist into action. Most importantly, develop a clear plan for teaching all your expectations, and plan for time each day to reteach and reinforce these expectations so that your students know exactly what is expected from the first day. Remember that establishing your prevention-focused classroom management plan is essential for both you and your students' success this year. It will lay a strong foundation for a positive classroom climate, positive relationships, and academic success.

This is also a good time to build your support system, set realistic goals, establish work-life balance, and become a lifelong learner. Following are some tips for settling into your new role:

♦ Connect with experienced and new teachers and other members of the school community. Learn names early on and identify some potential informal mentors. The front office staff is often an invaluable resource, and they likely have experience helping new teachers get started.

♦ Spend time learning about your school community, particularly if the area is new to you. Make plans to connect early on with your students' families and remember to make your first interaction with parents and guardians a positive one. Decide how you will communicate with families throughout the year.

♦ In addition to your classroom schedule, be sure to create your own daily schedule and stick to routines that promote mental and physical health and wellness. Remember that maintaining favorite activities like exercising, keeping up with a hobby, and spending time with friends and family is not a luxury; it is a necessity.

♦ Be sure to focus on your own social and emotional development. Practice self-awareness and emotion regulation. Reframe challenges as learning opportunities and intentionally practice having a growth mindset. Be patient with yourself and others and focus on what is within your control.

♦ Nurture your developing practice and remember that, as a teacher, you are a lifelong learner. Consider keeping a written or verbal journal to reflect on the year's successes and challenges. Attend required school district professional development opportunities and seek out free webinars and collaborative networks to expand your knowledge and to keep up with changes and trends in education.

Perspectives in Practice: A Novice Teacher on the Importance of a Predictable, Welcoming Learning Environment

Morgan is a new teacher in the fourth-grade classroom, fresh out of student teaching. Even in the first few months of her job as a full-fledged teacher, she has seen how well her student teaching experiences have prepared her to foster a predictable, welcoming environment. Morgan illustrates this when speaking about her students' participation in class.

Morgan explained that, at the beginning of the school year, none of her students would raise their hands to ask questions. All was well until they turned in their first quiz and only about half of the questions were answered correctly. All Morgan could think was, *where were all these questions earlier?*

By her fourth month of teaching, the majority of Morgan's students were asking questions and participating in extra practice activities. So, what changed? Since the start of the school year, Morgan has been building a welcoming, proactive, and predictable learning environment. It started in the very first week of class when she taught her students to reply to her "class class" with "yes yes" when she needed their attention. Morgan also scheduled intentionally, avoiding lessons like math right before lunch when the kids might be hungry and have more difficulty concentrating. If there is a change to the schedule, Morgan tells her students a day in advance. Every day when the students come in, they have a morning message and directions for their first activity posted on the board, so that way they know, "I come in, I read the board, and I do what it says."

All of these methods provide a predictable structure to Morgan's classroom. But Morgan strives for more than predictability; she also wants a classroom that is a positive, welcoming space for her students. By bringing her sense of humor into the classroom, her students see how she can turn a mistake into a joke, fix it, and move on. "And that helps the students a lot," Morgan says, "because for them to see 'Oh wait, my teacher makes mistakes too, and it's okay. And she's not upset, and she's not mad, and everything's fine' is super impactful." Then her students learn that when they make mistakes, no one will laugh at them, and the teacher won't get mad at them. She also helps students to regulate their emotions. For example, when they feel frustrated, she reminds them, "Well, you don't understand it *yet*, but you're going to, and I'm going to help you."

Morgan nurtures positivity in her classroom by encouraging open communication with a daily check-in that she calls CQC (Celebrations, Questions, and Concerns). Every morning, she invites her students to share what's on their minds to get them used to talking to each other about something that's personal rather than academic. She also uses this as a time to teach her students about how to appropriately react to and support each other, whether that's giving their classmate a smile and thumbs up or using a special hand signal to convey "me too" to someone expressing their concern. All these techniques reflect the understanding Morgan gained as a student teacher, which helped prepare her for when it was time to single-handedly take on a classroom.

Though only about halfway through the school year, Morgan's students have adapted to her classroom and are learning that it's okay to laugh at themselves. In addition, they show increased participation, and they are actively learning to be a community of open communicators. All these practices help Morgan create a predictable, welcoming classroom environment that engenders the success of her budding fourth graders.

Mentorship Corner: Supporting a Successful Transition

Tips for Cooperating Teachers

- ♦ As a mentor to your student teacher, you can play a pivotal role in supporting the transition from student teacher to first-year classroom teacher. Consider reviewing and offering feedback on job application materials, such as the cover letter, resume, and portfolio. Assistance may be needed with organization, highlighting the most relevant teaching experiences, and preparing for interviews.

If possible, ask a school or district administrator to meet with your student teacher to provide additional feedback and conduct a mock interview.

Tips for University Supervisors

- University supervisors can connect student teachers with campus career centers so they can learn about job opportunities and receive guidance on the job search process. Consider organizing study groups for certification exams as well as interview practice sessions for all student teachers.
- Encourage your student teacher to "cast a wide net" and be open to a variety of positions. While they may feel most comfortable in a teaching position very similar to their student teaching position, a narrow focus may be limiting. Perhaps student teachers can observe in other classrooms to get a sense of similarities and differences across grade levels so that they can better envision themselves in a variety of roles.
- As your student teacher begins to navigate the job search process and eventually begins their first year of teaching, check-in to provide support. You will be a useful sounding board and trusted professional resource as they navigate these challenging and exciting next steps.

Practice and Reflect: Application Activities to Support Your Development

Student Teacher: Consider the following questions for reflection and discussion:

Teaching Practice and Growth

- What were some of your most successful moments this semester, and what did you do to make them a success?
- Talk about a time that something didn't go as planned? How did you respond in the moment, and what did you learn from it?
- How did you grow in your application of effective classroom management practices? Why do you think this is often a challenging area for new teachers?
- Which teaching methods or strategies do you feel most confident using?
- What new skills or knowledge have you gained during your student teaching?

Student Relationships and Impact

- What was one memorable interaction you had with a student? How did it shape your perspective on teaching?
- How did you build relationships with students and foster a positive classroom environment?
- In what ways do you think you made an impact on your students' learning and growth?

Collaboration and Professionalism

- What did you learn from working with your cooperating teacher and other colleagues?
- How did you collaborate with families, and what did you learn from those interactions?
- How did you approach feedback from your cooperating teacher and university supervisor, and how did it help you improve?

Inclusivity and Equity

- How did you incorporate inclusive practices into your teaching?
- What challenges did you face in meeting the diverse needs of your students, and how did you address them?
- How have your beliefs about equity and inclusion evolved during your student teaching experience?

Self-Reflection and Looking Forward

- What are you most proud of from your student teaching experience?
- What areas do you still want to grow in as a teacher?
- What advice would you give to future student teachers based on your experience?

Teacher Toolbox: Resources for Further Exploration

1. Certification Guidance:
    a. We Are Teachers: Your Guide to Teacher Certification Exams in Every State[1]
2. Interview Guidance:
    a. Edutopia: 11 Questions You will be asked at a Teaching Interview[2]
    b. EdWeek: 5 Essential Questions Teachers Should Ask at an Interview[3]

3. Digication is a platform for ePortfolios:
    a. Blog Post: The Importance of Reflection and Advocacy in Teacher Education with Janet VanLone (author)[4]
    b. Example Digication Portfolio: Lainey Lavelle, Early Childhood Education Major at Bucknell University[5]
4. Portfolio Guidance:
    a. We Are Teachers: How to Create a Teaching Portfolio (Examples & Free Templates)[6]

Notes

1. https://www.weareteachers.com/teacher-certification-exams/
2. https://www.edutopia.org/article/11-questions-youll-be-asked-teaching-interview/
3. https://www.edweek.org/jobs/5-essential-questions-teachers-should-ask-during-job-interviews/2021/06?utm_source=goog&utm_medium=cpc&utm_campaign=tsj+jobseeker-content&s_kwcid=AL!6416!3!581096335875!b!!g!!teacher%20interview&gad_source=1&gclid=CjwKCAiAnKi8BhB0EiwA58DA4cmV-ZuBkaUvSKjuFgm-gjVWUJZgjLzruvKMq3k1UUuECwPqrdwfbBoCOzYQAvD_BwE
4. https://www.digication.com/blog/reflection-advocacy-teacher-education
5. https://bucknell.digication.com/laineylavelle/home
6. https://www.weareteachers.com/teaching-portfolio-examples/

References

Agyapong, B., Obuobi-Donkor, G., Burback, L., & Wei, Y. (2022). Stress, burnout, anxiety and depression among teachers: A scoping review. *International Journal of Environmental Research and Public Health, 19*(17), 10706. https://doi.org/10.3390/ijerph191710706

Altan, M. Z., & Sağlamel, H. (2015). Student teaching from the perspectives of cooperating teachers and pupils. *Cogent Education, 2*(1). https://doi.org/10.1080/2331186X.2015.1086291

Flower, A., McKenna, J. W., & Haring, C. D. (2016). Behavior and classroom management: Are teacher preparation programs really preparing our teachers? *Preventing School Failure: Alternative Education for Children and Youth, 61*(2), 163–169. https://doi.org/10.1080/1045988X.2016.1231109

García, E., & Weiss, E. (2019). *The teacher shortage is real, large and growing, and worse than we thought.* Economic Policy Institute. https://www.epi.org/files/pdf/163651.pdf

Ingersoll, R. M., & Tran, H. (2023). Teacher shortages and turnover in rural schools in the US: An organizational analysis. *Educational Administration Quarterly, 59*(2), 396–431. https://doi.org/10.1177/0013161X231159922

Johnson, D. D. (2021). Predictors of teachers' turnover and transfer intentions: A multiple mediation model of teacher engagement. *Journal of Education Human Resources, 39*(3), 322–349.

Meristo, M., & Eisenschmidt, E. (2014). Novice teachers' perceptions of school climate and self-efficacy. *International Journal of Educational Research, 67*, 1–10. https://doi.org/10.1016/j.ijer.2014.04.003

Oliver, P. V. (2024). Perfectionism and stress during student teaching: Managing uncertainty with overcompensation. *Journal of Educational Research and Practice, 14*, 23–36, https://doi.org/10.5590/JERAP.2024.14.1.02

Stevenson, N. A., VanLone, J., & Barber, B. R. (2020). A commentary on the misalignment of teacher education and the need for classroom behavior management skills. *Education and Treatment of Children, 43*(4), 393–404. https://doi.org/10.1007/s43494-020-00031-1

Suzuki, W. (2021). *Good anxiety: Harnessing the power of the most misunderstood emotion.* Simon and Schuster.

Won, N., Liu, K., & Bukko, D. (2019). Developing instructional skills: Perspectives of feedback in student teaching. *Networks: An Online Journal for Teacher Research, 21* (2). https://doi.org/10.4148/2470-6353.1303

Zito, S., Petrovic, J., Böke, B. N., Sadowski, I., Carsley, D., & Heath, N. L. (2024). Exploring the stress management and well-being needs of pre-service teachers. *Teaching and Teacher Education, 152*, 104805. https://doi.org/10.1016/j.tate.2024.104805

APPENDIX A: CLASSROOM PRACTICES IMPLEMENTATION PLAN: REMINDERS FOR STARTING YOUR TEACHING CAREER

Directions: The purpose of this assignment is to develop a comprehensive classroom management plan. You will have this plan to review when it comes to plan for your first years of teaching. Your plan should include the following sections:

1. *Philosophy of classroom and behavior management*: Write a 1–2 page narrative outlining your beliefs about classroom management and the type of classroom environment you want to create. Why is this important for you and for your future students? (all chapters).
2. *Prevention strategies*: Develop/teach classroom routines and expectations, revise and include your matrix, using prevention-focused teacher behaviors (see Chapter 3).
3. *Instructional strategies*: connection between instruction and classroom management, teacher behaviors to support good instruction and classroom management, developing lesson plans (see Chapters 5 and 6).
4. *Class-wide strategies*: Describe specific class-wide strategies you plan to implement in your classroom (see Chapter 3).
5. *Intensifying support strategies*: How will you support students in need of increased support? Include examples (see Chapter 4).
6. *Strategies for monitoring your implementation of effective practices*: How will you monitor your own implementation of these strategies? (~1–2 paragraphs).
7. Strategies for monitoring your own emotional state, self-care, and finding support (see Chapters 1 and 8).
8. *Getting off to a great start*: A reminder checklist for your first weeks of schools (all chapters).

For Product Safety Concerns and Information please contact our EU
representative GPSR@taylorandfrancis.com
Taylor & Francis Verlag GmbH, Kaufingerstraße 24, 80331 München, Germany

www.ingramcontent.com/pod-product-compliance
Lightning Source LLC
Chambersburg PA
CBHW051646230426